Sherpas:
Reflections on Change
in Himalayan Nepal

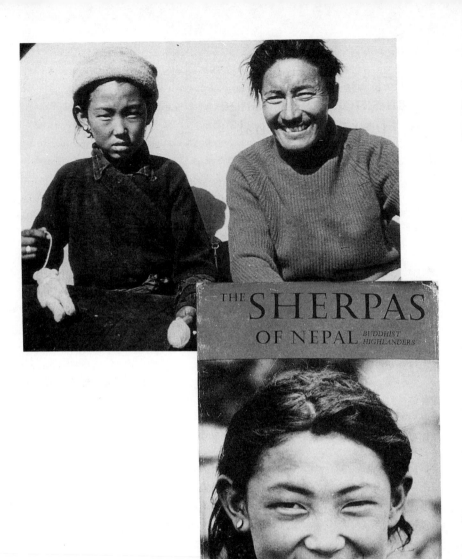

THE SHERPAS
OF NEPAL BUDDHIST HIGHLANDERS

SHERPAS

Reflections on Change
in Himalayan Nepal

James F. Fisher
With a Foreword by Sir Edmund Hillary

UNIVERSITY OF
CALIFORNIA PRESS

Berkeley
Los Angeles
Oxford

Title page: Ang Phute, from Namche Bazaar. She is shown first aged twelve in 1953, seated at Tengboche Monastery beside Tenzing Norgay a few weeks before he made the first ascent of Mt. Everest with Edmund Hillary. In 1957 Christoph von Fürer-Haimendorf photographed her during the fieldwork that resulted in his monograph *The Sherpas of Nepal.* The photograph was used on the back of the book's dust jacket. Later Ang Phute married out of caste a Kathmandu Newar, a businessman whose wealth increased after he obtained the Nepal franchise for Toyota. The next photograph was taken in 1974, in Kathmandu, and the last in 1986, several years after Ang Phute's divorce had left her a wealthy woman. Although the most recent photograph shows her wearing an elegant Tibetan dress made of Chinese brocade, her preferred attire was more casual. Ang Phute's children know Nepali and English and have been educated in the United States. They do not speak either Sherpa or Newari.

University of California Press
Berkeley and Los Angeles, California

University of California Press, Ltd.
Oxford, England

Library of Congress Cataloging-in-Publication Data

Fisher, James F.
    Sherpas : reflections on change in Himalayan Nepal / James F.
Fisher ; with a foreword by Sir Edmund Hillary.
        p.   cm.
    Includes bibliographical references.
    ISBN 0-520-06770-3 (alk. paper).—ISBN 0-520-06941-2 (pbk. :
alk. paper)
    1. Sherpas.   2. Solu-Khumbu (Nepal)—Description and travel.
3. Education—Nepal—Solu-Khumbu.   4. Tourist trade—Nepal—
Solu-Khumbu.   I. Title.
DS493.9.S5F57 1990
915.496—dc20   89-27155

Printed in the United States of America

1 2 3 4 5 6 7 8 9

The paper used in this publication meets the minimum requirements
of American National Standard for Information Sciences—
Permanence of Paper for Printed Library Materials, ANSI Z39.48-
1984. ⊗

For Catherine

Contents

Foreword

I warmed to Jim Fisher the first time I met him. I expected him as a Peace Corps member to be idealistic and possibly a little impractical, but he seemed to be able to handle most things very effectively—and there was no doubting his tremendous enthusiasm. And what an eater he was! On the basic hill diet of rice and dal he was the unbeatable champion. Even the Sherpas sat and watched with wide-eyed amazement.

Jim was prepared to undertake almost any task at all—it was immaterial if he knew much about it. Off he would go, and after a series of adventures or near disasters he would somehow battle through to a satisfactory conclusion. He even managed to put up with the typical jokes of the largely New Zealand team, and we quickly learned to accept him as a sensible and agreeable human being.

Perhaps this was Jim Fisher's greatest strength: he got on well with everyone—Sherpas, New Zealanders, Indians, Englishmen—and he was always kind and generous. Jim rapidly became absorbed into the Sherpa community. He was never a cold, calculating observer accumulating data with no feeling or motivation of a warm relationship. Jim sensed the desires and needs of these hardy mountain people and accepted (and recorded) their strengths and their weaknesses. He learned to share their laughter and their sorrows, their ambitions and their grim determination to survive.

My motivation was perhaps simpler than Jim's. I was doing what the Sherpas wanted us to do, be it building a school, a hospital, or a bridge—that was reason enough for me. But Jim was also eager to understand the influence that schools and tourism were having on the traditional life of the Sherpas. He wanted to know if the changes were good or bad. What was the future of the Sherpas, he wondered, and of their culture and religion? In this book he expresses his carefully considered conclusions.

Sir Edmund Hillary

Acknowledgments

This book is the result of discussions with so many people and research spread over so many years that it is difficult to pinpoint and thank all those who have helped me formulate my scattered observations into a coherent statement. Sir Edmund Hillary's invitation to join the Himalayan Schoolhouse Expedition fueled my interest in the Sherpas and made the entire subsequent research program possible. He has been unceasingly kind and helpful over the years, even when I have strayed far from Solu-Khumbu on research trips elsewhere in the Himalayas. Three students at Carleton College—Pamela Falkenberg, Debby Cornfield, and Michele Curtis—have incorporated some of my education data into their research papers, and I have benefited from their discussions. In 1978 Tracey Abman and Lynn Stephens, also Carleton students, accompanied me to Khumbu as research assistants, funded by the National Science Foundation. They collected much of the information on tourism. Two more Carleton students, D. Kendall RePass and Steve McGraw, read an advanced version of the manuscript and offered excellent suggestions for its improvement.

During long periods of residence in Kathmandu I have sought the advice of many friends with diverse experience in Khumbu or Nepal. Most of what I know about Nepal in general, as well as much of what I know about the Sherpas in particular, I learned from Dor Bahadur Bista. Barbara Brower, Brot Coburn, Robin Houston, Jean Meadowcroft, and Stan Stevens have each read at least one chapter of the manuscript and have given me the benefit of their extensive knowledge. Elizabeth Hawley drew from her incomparable expeditionary lore to provide the statistics on Sherpa mountaineering deaths and ascents of Everest. Bruce and Margaret Jefferies provided many facts and figures on tourism and mountaineering. Robin Houston generously made available his taped interviews with eight eminent sardars. Frances Klatzel, who helped the Tengboche rimpoche (as Ngawang Tenzin Zangbu, the reincarnate abbot of Tengboche, is normally called; rimpoche is an honorific title given to a reincarnate lama) bring the Tengboche Cultural Center into existence, brought me up to date on developments at the monastery. The Winrock International Foundation and the Human Resources Center (both in Kathmandu) allowed me frequent use of their computer facilities.

Harka Gurung and Chaitanya Mishra read the entire manuscript and provided criticism and helpful suggestions. John Draper also read the manuscript and offered pages of insightful and detailed comments, criticisms, and corrections. Dhruba Koirala drew the maps.

On American shores, Charles Houston, a member of the first Western party to visit Khumbu (in 1950) provided, by mail and by phone, a penetrating critique of the manuscript and generously gave me his pictures from the 1950 trip to use in this book. Catherine C. Fisher, the late Frank L. Fisher, Kim C. Fisher, Sarah O'Dowd, and Nancy C. Wilkie helped me to clarify the flow of the first chapter. Mac Odell raised useful questions of interpretation and format.

The staff of the University of California Press were unfailingly helpful, particularly my editor, Lynne Withey, and Stephanie Fay, who meticulously copyedited the manuscript.

I owe the greatest debt of all to the Sherpas with whom over the years I have lived and trekked and climbed and discussed the issues raised here. They are far too many to list individually, but I should single out at least my old friend Sardar Mingma Tsering and his wife, Ang Doli, for their hospitality on the many occasions I have stayed at their Khunde house. I also thank the abbot of Tengboche Monastery for many long and frank discussions and Shyam Pradhan, perennial principal of the Khumjung School, who has always thoughtfully answered my queries about education.

Mr. Mingma Norbu Sherpa and Mr. Lhakpa Norbu Sherpa gave me the benefit of their unparalleled knowledge of Sherpa life and of the workings of Sagarmatha National Park, of which they are both former wardens; critiques like theirs, informed by both native intuition and Western training, are unprecedented in Khumbu scholarship, and I am enormously grateful to them.

The book could never have been written without the unfailing help, insightful advice, and astute observations of Mr. Ang Rita Sherpa. In 1974 Ang Rita accompanied me and my family to Khumbu and served for several months there as my research assistant and translator (I speak Nepali but only a smattering of Sherpa). Since then he has spent long periods patiently answering a steady stream of questions, often by mail, and collecting protocols for the chapter on ethnographic futures. My debt to him is incalculable.

I should add finally that if I had accepted all the constructive suggestions offered by my friends and colleagues, this would be a flawless book; as it is I can only profusely thank all of them for their help.

All the photographs in the book are mine unless otherwise credited. No part of the book has been published previously, with the exception of an early version of chapter 4, which appeared under the title "Tourists and Sherpas" in *Contributions to Nepalese Studies* 14, no. 1 (1986).

Finally, I am grateful to the following institutions for generously supporting the research on which the book is based: The Wenner-Gren Foundation (Grant-in-Aid); the National Science Foundation (Grant No. SER77-06304); the Social Science Research Council; and Carleton College for its characteristically strong support in the form of various faculty research and writing awards.

Note on Orthography and Sherpa Names

It is anomalous that no accepted convention exists for writing the language of a group as famous, well studied, and thoroughly documented as the Sherpas. Because Sherpa, unlike closely related Tibetan, is not a written language, there are no indigenous texts that could be used to generate a systematic transliteration into roman letters. I have therefore had to settle for the same method others have used, namely, to write Sherpa words as close to the way they sound as possible and to check these phonetic renderings with native speakers of Sherpa who also speak, read, and write Nepali and English.

But there is no clear-cut solution to the linguistic conundrums posed by this orthographic task. For instance, I use *gompa*, glossed as "temple, monastery," because this transliteration is closer to the original Tibetan (the conventional, letter-for-letter scholarly version would be *dgon-pa*) than *gomba*, which others have used. Neither spelling, however, approximates the spoken Sherpa equivalent, "gonda." I use the Tibetan word only because of its more general familiarity to those interested in Tibetan Buddhism. Similarly, I refer to Rongbuk (rather than the more phonetically faithful Rumbu) Monastery.

Place names pose their own difficulties. The village I spell Khunde others have written Kunde, but neither spelling reflects the pronunciation of the word when it is written in Tibetan script—Khumte, meaning the upper (*te*) Khum, as opposed to Khumjung, the Khum located on a flat place at a lower elevation (*jung*). As for Khumjung, Ortner (1989) reports that Hari Ram, an Indian explorer who made the first recorded visit to Khumbu by a foreigner, in 1885, called it Khumbu Dzong (Khumbu fort). Although this sort of name is common in Tibetan-speaking areas, it seems etymologically odd here since there is no structure in Khumjung remotely resembling a fort. Whether Hari Ram's rendering, or my own, is a folk etymology, I do not know.

In any case, Sherpas believe that "Khumte" must have been the original correct pronunciation, since it has a recognizable meaning, rather than "Khunde," which they regard as a corruption of the pristine term. But "Khunde" is invariably the spoken form and hence the spelling I use here.

• • •

All Sherpas have dual names, one element of which is often the day of the week on which they are born:

> Monday   Dawa (Da)
> Tuesday   Mingma
> Wednesday   Lhakpa
> Thursday   Phurba (Prua)
> Friday   Pasang
> Saturday   Pemba
> Sunday   Nima

Such a name may be followed by a second name, such as Tsering, meaning "long life," giving combinations like Mingma Tsering; or it may be preceded by Ang, meaning "young," resulting in names like Ang Nima. Because the number of such compounds is small, several individuals often share the same name. In this book alone, for example, which contains relatively few Sherpa names, there are four Ang Tserings and two Ang Ritas.

Foreigners tend to keep individuals with duplicate names straight by specifying locality: for example, the Khumjung Ang Rita versus the Khunde Ang Rita. Sherpas distinguish them by specifying locality or clan or some other relationship: for example, the Ang Rita who is the son of Mingma Tsering versus the Ang Rita who is the son of Kappa Kalden.

Sherpas do not normally have a "last name." When they live elsewhere in Nepal or travel to foreign countries, the word *Sherpa* begins functioning as a last name, as on passports or on school registration forms. But this is a modern affectation without foundation in Solu-Khumbu, where such a system would give everyone the same last name.

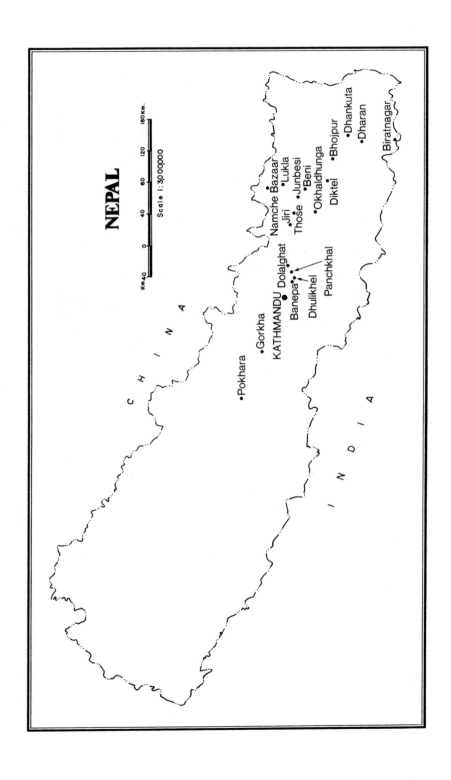

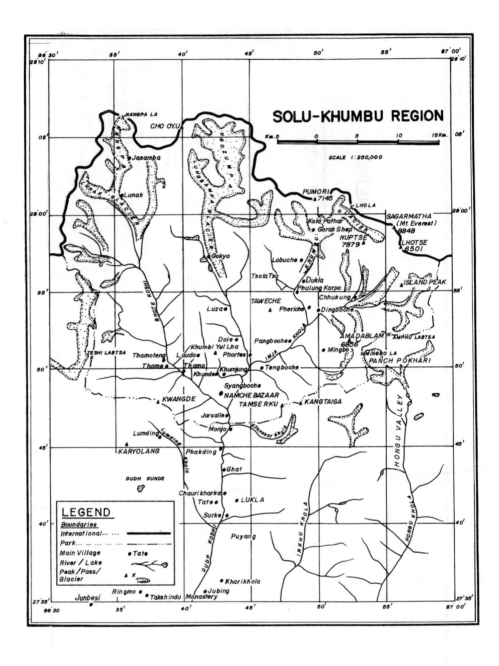

SOLU-KHUMBU REGION

SCALE 1:250,000

LEGEND

Boundaries
International... ...
Park... ... ...
Main Village   • Tate
River / Lake
Peak /Pass/
Glacier   ▲ X

Satellite view of Solu-Khumbu. © 1990 DRL West Germany.

Introduction:
Monograph, Memoir, Confession

This book is neither an anthropological monograph in the technical sense, nor a memoir with literary pretensions, nor a picture book in the coffee-table tradition. I have tried instead to devise a multivocal format that incorporates elements of all these genres, one that will interest anthropologists, mountaineers, and trekkers to the Mt. Everest region of Nepal and development planners and others interested in the phenomenon of sudden change in this once remote, still stunningly beautiful area. Neither a traditional ethnography nor a history of the Sherpas nor a psychological portrait of them,[1] this book traces the impact on contemporary Sherpa society of modern education and mass tourism and assesses the Sherpas' views of their collective future. It is a story of many things happening in a very short time.

The account covers three periods when I lived in Solu-Khumbu, the first in 1964 when, as a member of the Himalayan Schoolhouse Expedition, I participated in building many of the facilities and institutions whose impact I returned to observe in 1974 and 1978. Final research and writing were done in Kathmandu in 1985–86, with a brief trip to fill in some photographic gaps in 1988. The total time I spent in Solu-Khumbu was a little more than a year.

I suspect I have always been an anthropologist at heart, even before I understood what the word meant. But I began studying anthropology as a graduate student at the University of Chicago (having majored in philosophy as an undergraduate) only after my return to the United States in 1965 at the conclusion of the Schoolhouse Expedition. There is a reflexive sense, then, in which this book is an analysis of my pre-anthropological life in the Everest area, and to that extent it is a book by myself about myself. But if Geertz (1973, 346) is correct in saying that much of what passes as ethnography is merely confession, it is no novel claim to describe this book as part memoir.

In 1974, ten years after the Schoolhouse Expedition, I returned to study the impact of the elementary schools we had built in the Sherpa villages. The Sherpa villages of Solu-Khumbu are perhaps unique in Nepal in being situated near indigenous pedagogical institutions—Buddhist monasteries. In 1964 Dor Bahadur Bista, who had observed the mindless destruction of Buddhist temples in Thakkhola by educated Thakalis in the early 1960s, alerted me to the potentially destructive sociological implications of such ostensibly benign institutions as village schools (see Bista 1971). In 1964 I observed not only that the village schools and the monasteries were teaching different subjects—science, mathematics, English, and so forth as opposed to religious subjects—but also that they were doing so in unrelated languages written in different scripts—Nepali in the schools and Tibetan in the monasteries. Would the two institutions, I wondered abstractly, compete as the locus of literacy?

When I looked at the situation "on the ground" in 1974, whatever apparent impact the schools had had seemed swamped by the flood of tourists that had overrun Khumbu. The anthropologist Ralph Beals once wrote that as an effective agent of change, one road is worth a thousand schools. The same might be said for one STOL (short-take-off-and-landing) airstrip. For in 1964 we had also leveled some jungle and a few potato fields at a deservedly obscure Sherpa hamlet called Lukla to make a ten-degree slope long enough to accommodate a small single-engine aircraft. Our hardheaded intention—to provide more direct access to Khumbu so that Sir Edmund Hillary could more effectively get supplies to the hospital he intended to build in the village of Khunde—seems naive in retrospect. Neither he nor I had the remotest inkling that the airstrip would soon become a major conduit for tourists and would spark a burgeoning, radically new industry in Khumbu.

Lukla airstrip stands today as a monument to the distinction between manifest (or intended) and latent functions. Tourists cared little for the manifest function we had in mind and supplanted it with a latent function that has become the airstrip's only function. The first Westerners to see Khumbu were the Houston-Tilman party in 1950; in 1964 only twenty outsiders visited the area, which was then a fourteen-day walk from Banepa, sixteen miles east of Kathmandu. In 1974, however, with Kathmandu–Khumbu travel time reduced to forty minutes, about 3,500 outsiders, I was astonished to discover, visited Khumbu (by 1986 that number had almost doubled). I therefore returned in the fall of 1978 to examine in more detail what tourism had done for, or to, the Sherpas.

The problems were evident enough, but gradually it occurred to me that foreigners' worries about impending doom in Khumbu did not adequately take into account Sherpa perceptions of either their own interests or their major problems in the middle-range future. So in 1986 I returned once again to study the Sherpas' concerns about the future and the resolutions they envisioned for these problems.

The book begins where I began with Sherpas: the Himalayan School-house Expedition of 1964. Chapter 1 gives an impressionistic and idio-syncratic picture of Sherpa society as I saw it, in all my callow naïveté, in those pretourist days. It also provides some of the flavor and fervor of the nonmountaineering side of what developed into an institution in its own right: the multifaceted Hillary expedition of the 1960s and 1970s. It has no pretensions to being a "base-line study," and I leave it to contemporary visitors to compare their own experiences of Khumbu with my archival account of that vanished world.

Chapter 2 backtracks, giving a brief history of Sherpa society as it had developed by the early 1960s, and then outlines the major periods of recent change and contact with the outside world. Chapter 3 deals with the impact on Sherpa life of the schools that were built in the 1960s. Chapter 4 discusses the unintended result of the airstrip we built at Lukla: the advent of tourism. I chart its consequences for Sherpas and for tourists. Chapter 5 is an attempt to project the ethnographic future—that is, to describe the problems of the medium-range future as seen by a cross section of Sherpas. Chapter 6 briefly concludes and summarizes the discussion with an updated account of life in Khumbu today.

The photographs scattered throughout the text themselves constitute a dismembered chapter. Their purpose is to document many of the before-and-after phenomena described in the book. Some of the pic-tures may be pretty, but if they are, it is because the people and places of Solu-Khumbu are so visually arresting that it is difficult to take un-appealing pictures of them. My aim is not to add to the already copious supply of books filled with glossy prints of Himalayan places and people. Rather, my photographs have a point: to show with an immediacy that prose (my prose, at least) cannot capture how some of the substantive changes I describe look with the words torn off them.

Most of the book is based on my own research and experiences in Solu-Khumbu, especially Khumbu proper (Namche Bazaar and the villages above it), but I have borrowed freely, especially in chapter 2, from the work of other observers of the Sherpas. Chief among them are the scholarly books and articles of my friends Christoph von Fürer-Haimendorf, Michael Oppitz, Sherry Ortner, and Robert Paul. Individually and, even more, collectively, their work is so estimable that I should explain why yet another book is even necessary. (Not without reason has Sir Edmund Hillary described Khumbu as "the most surveyed, examined, blood-taken, anthropologically dissected area in the world" [Rowell 1980].)[2] Fürer-Haimendorf's recent book *The Sherpas Transformed,* for example, covers much of the same ground that I cover here, but from a more nostalgic point of view, in which current developments compare unfavorably with the good old days of the 1950s described in his original, pioneering, ethnography *The Sherpas of Nepal,* on which all subsequent scholarship has depended. (Westerners do not have a monopoly on romanticizing the past: Sherpas consider Khumbu to have been a *beyul,* "hidden valley," a sanctuary from the troubled outside world.) At the opposite literary pole, Ortner's and Paul's stimulating books (*Sherpas Through Their Rituals* and *The Tibetan Symbolic World: Psychoanalytic Explorations,* respectively) present Sherpa culture at such a remote level that few, if any, Sherpas would be able to recognize them as grounded in their own experience of life. (Ortner's *High Religion: A Cultural and Political History of Sherpa Buddhism,* which I read only after this book was essentially finished, will provide readers hungry for knowledge of Sherpa history and religion a delicious feast.)[3]

On the "development" side I have waded through the many reports, surveys, and memoranda written in connection with such projects as Sagarmatha National Park, hydroelectric dams, and conservation efforts of all sorts. Running through this literature (and through the conversation of its authors) is an "expert" attitude with occasional pretensions to omniscience. A succession of visiting foreigners (Americans, New Zealanders, British, and Germans, among others, and now, increasingly, Nepalese officials) has concluded characteristically brief Khumbu visits with definitive pronouncements, delivered with unnerving aplomb, outlining solutions to problems in the area. That the advice of these experts often either perpetuates the questionable assumptions of previous visitors or is mutually contradictory does not deter them from giving it.

The more I sifted through all this well-intentioned literature, the more I thought that it was time to hear directly from the Sherpas themselves. Faced with lacunae on both the academic and development sides, I intend here to describe change as the Sherpas see and experience it. Of course at one level such a goal is sheer illusion: this study, like all others, is only one more foreigner's attempt to penetrate the ostensibly open Khumbu world. Certainly my own analysis and judgments inform the entire book—after all, I wrote it. But I attempt throughout to let the Sherpas speak for themselves whenever possible. While investigating education, for example, I asked children to write essays, which I read to assess the attitudes and values they were forming. And as a complement to unilateral pronouncements (my own included) on the various ecological and other difficulties the area faces, I asked adult Sherpas to tell me what they thought would be the main problems they would have to face in twenty-five years. I should add that the problems inherent in studying education and the future in this way were much greater than I had anticipated; nobody really knows how to do it yet.

A final note of clarification: When I refer to the influence of tourism, I usually include in that term the phenomenon of mountaineering. Only 2 percent of Khumbu visitors are members of mountaineering expeditions, but such expeditions usually employ a disproportionately large number of Sherpas. An exception to this rule is the recent trend among climbers to dispense with Sherpas entirely and climb the mountain under their own steam. Over the years I have come to think of mountaineering and tourism as not just related but the same, the differences between them being increasingly in degree rather than in kind. Although this view will undoubtedly horrify many of my mountaineering friends (but not, I think, the Sherpas), the enormous increase in the popularity of mountaineering and of trekking in the last few years means that there is frequently no longer any useful way to distinguish them. Tourists cross high passes and climb peaks that a few years ago only a party of experienced mountaineers would have attempted. One of the foremost American climbers, Mike Covington, once told me that the only difference between the expeditions he joins and those he guides is that on the latter he is paid and on the former he is not. He predicted that it was just a matter of time before Everest would be a guided peak.

CHAPTER I

The Himalayan Schoolhouse Expedition, 1964

As a self-proclaimed science, anthropology until recently paid little attention to the personal impact of the field experience on the observer— how the raw conditions of life in some remote corner of the world affected the anthropologist's life and, especially, observations and conclusions. Fieldwork in highly stratified Asian societies is so complicated by people's hiding behind masks, to help them play the role they want the world to think they normally play, that something akin to the Heisenberg uncertainty principle exists: we can scarcely be sure that what we see is not an artifact of our presence rather than the routine day-to-day unfolding of what is "naturally" there (see Berreman's 1962 description of how people in the Indian Himalayas fool outsiders).

The question of what impact an anthropologist has on the long-term development of a society, however, is also rarely raised, except in applied anthropology projects where that is the only issue that matters. In Nepal, no one has studied the later developments produced by his or her previous work, and for good reason: anthropologists normally have no long-term effects on a society, although the effects on the individuals an anthropologist comes to know particularly well can be enormous.

My case is a partial exception. As a member of the Himalayan Schoolhouse Expedition of 1964 (but not yet as a bona fide anthropologist), I was inextricably part of cataclysmic events that changed the face of Khumbu forever. This chapter, using excerpts from the diary I kept at that time, puts those events on record.

• • •

What had first attracted me to Nepal, in an unabashedly romantic way, was the Himalayas. I cannot recall how I first became interested in this impossibly distant mountain range—perhaps it was only the typical American fascination with whatever was the world's biggest, whether the genre was buildings or animals, cities or mountains. Had I known about the *Guinness Book of World Records,* I would have been an avid reader of it. I was intrigued by singular, preferably arcane, facts about our planet and could never resist *Ripley's Believe It or Not.* But for as long as I could remember I had read voraciously on the Himalayas— books on exploration, mountaineering, history, and what little existed on its peoples.

The book that had seized my imagination more than any other, to the point of briefly paralyzing any thoughts other than those devoted to figuring out a way to get to Nepal or Tibet, was James Hilton's *Lost Horizon.* Although the idea was never a fully conscious one, I suppose what I really was searching for in Nepal when I went there in 1962, as an English teacher in the first Peace Corps group, was Shangri-La and its benignly perfect people or at least a more equitable, less frenetically driven and materialistic society than the one I had just come from. Like many anthropologists, I was drawn to other cultures because I couldn't stand my own.

Much as I liked the Kathmandu Valley—its lush, verdant beauty and its warm, fascinating, hospitable people—it somehow fell short of Shangri-La. Maybe it just wasn't high enough. Anyway, from what I had read, if there were a Shangri-La anywhere, it must be in the Sherpa country—the fabled Solu-Khumbu area around Mt. Everest. But that was so far away and difficult to reach, and the Peace Corps in those first days was so timid about placing people where they couldn't be evacuated in medical emergencies, that the dream of being assigned there was an impossible one. Although to me the Peace Corps seemed unnecessarily cautious and conservative, in its own self-view the sheer political fact of its existence was a risk sufficiently bold unto the day.

Still, I knew that Sir Edmund Hillary had built a primary school in Khumjung (Fig. 1), the largest Sherpa village in Khumbu, and as an educator in Nepal, I was interested to know more about it. Having read in the newspaper that the conqueror of Everest was in town (his movements never escape public notice), I decided to track him down.

If the name Sir Edmund Hillary conjures up magic even for people

Fig. 1. Aerial view of the hour-glass villages (Sherpas think they resemble the body of a horse) of Khumjung (*below*) and Khunde (*above*), with the Japanese-built Everest-View Hotel set among the trees above and to the left of the villages. Still further left and out of sight over the hill lies Syangboche airstrip and, below Syangboche, Namche Bazaar. The high peak is Kwangde.

who see mountains merely as inconvenient aberrations in the earth's crust to be flown over as quickly as possible, it certainly is special to anyone who loves mountains high and low. As someone who has always felt an attraction to mountains and the thrill (including the fear) of being in high places—whether in a tree in my front yard in Kentucky, where I grew up, or on a steep face in the Rockies—I came quickly under his spell. My journal entry for December 20, 1962 (almost ten years after the Hillary-Tenzing ascent of Everest) tells how I found him at the bungalow of Charles Wylie, a military attaché at the British embassy.

I went to see if Hillary was there. He was and was seeing two gentlemen off in the driveway. I waited for about fifteen minutes while he talked to them; then they left. He walked toward the house (and me), and I stepped forward and introduced myself. I felt rather small, for he is a tall man—I'd say between six feet two inches and six feet five inches; his hair is rather long, especially in front, with a long shock falling down over his forehead, just as it did in the movie *The Ascent of Everest*. I told him I was interested in his school, and he said he would be glad to discuss it with me, so we talked there in the driveway for about a quarter of an hour. I asked him if he could use a Peace Corps teacher up there, and he said he didn't think the facilities would warrant it yet. Only elementary schools are involved, and they teach, according to Hillary, just "reading and writing," mostly of Nepali but also possibly of English. He said most of the Sherpas could speak Nepali, but few could read or write it. . . . They are not building schools in Namche Bazaar, the area's main town, partly because there is a school there already (but no teacher), partly because the need is greater in the other small villages; Hillary said Namche is now full of rogues, thieves, and other such people he described with unprintable adjectives; apparently the town is quite "commercialized" by now. Hillary was extremely nice and not at all arrogant or above talking to me, and I think we both enjoyed the conversation.

I had another long talk with him in June 1963 and wrote to him in November of that year, outlining my thoughts about the educational needs of the Sherpas in light of what I had learned by this time about education in Nepal. On November 20 I was standing on King's Way when Father Moran (the worldly, perennial, and primordial Jesuit priest who had started the Catholic secondary school in Kathmandu in the early 1950s) came roaring past in a battered van with the New Zealand mountaineers Mike Gill and Jim Wilson, the latter a graduate student in philosophy at Banaras Hindu University. Father Moran slammed on the brakes, and his other passenger, Sir Edmund, asked if I could stop by Charles Wylie's bungalow for tea at half past three. Sir Edmund had been favorably disposed toward the issues I had raised in my letter, but when we met later in the day he didn't refer to it specifically. In his typical decisive way, he had made up his mind quickly and just assumed from there on that I was "in." [1]

Would the Peace Corps buy the idea? The Peace Corps director, the indomitable and charismatic Willie Unsoeld, was in the United States having nine of his toes amputated (he kept one of his pinkies). They had become frostbitten during a bivouac above 28,000 feet on his descent of the southeast ridge following his epic traverse of Everest via the west ridge. [2] His replacement, Bill Warren, took a bold and idealistic (and reckless, in the view of Washington bureaucrats, who later fired him over another issue) approach to the Peace Corps and immediately approved a six-month extension of my Peace Corps service as a member of the Hillary team.

The plan was for me to accompany the New Zealanders Jim and Ann Wilson to Khumbu in April 1964. I would stay there until August, evaluating the schools already in operation (Khumjung, Pangboche, and Thame), making recommendations for improvements, and helping to prepare building sites for new schools in Junbesi, Chaurikharka, and Namche Bazaar. I would return to Kathmandu at the end of the summer and march back to Khumbu in the fall with the main expedition, which would build the schools, a couple of bridges, and an airstrip and would climb a mountain for good measure.

In the meantime I became the local de facto expedition organizer, opening a bank account in Hillary's and my names, storing and sorting equipment, and obtaining permission for the expedition from the Foreign Office in Singha Durbar.[3] Singha Durbar, an ornate English-style stucco palace with a thousand ostentatiously furnished rooms, was once the prime minister's private residence. But after the revolution of 1950 overthrew the Ranas (the family that had provided the prime ministers), it became the center of His Majesty's Government.

Even at this early date I began thinking of the effects that building all these schools might have on Sherpa society. I had no doubt that our agenda was positive, but would there also be hidden cultural costs? During the winter I went to Calcutta to visit Desmond Doig, a bon vivant journalist and a veteran of two Hillary expeditions to Khumbu who had a passionate interest in the Sherpas and their life-style. He shared my worries about the future and groused enough about what was already happening in Khumbu to confirm my belief that this aspect of the project needed more thought than it had yet received. I resolved to give these concerns high priority.

Everything threatened to fall apart when I was abruptly hospitalized a day before the Wilsons arrived from Banaras in mid-April. The diagnosis, infectious mononucleosis, gave me the unsought and unwanted distinction of being the first officially recognized and recorded such case in Nepal's medical history. The cure prescribed was flat-on-my-back rest. After moping and generally feeling sorry for myself for three weeks, I was finally released from the hospital in early May.

A week later I had an audience with His Majesty King Mahendra (a royal audience was granted to all members of the first Peace Corps group at the end of our tour of duty) and told him of my plans to work in Khumbu. As the first monarch to travel extensively in the remoter areas of the country, he expressed interest in my project. On May 15 I set out in a race against the monsoon, trying to make up some of the precious time I had already lost. A four-wheel-drive jeep barely got me as far as the Newar bazaar town of Dhulikhel; from there a series of double-time marches pushed me and my Sherpa assistant, Phurba Tenzing, over the Lamjura-Bhanjyang (a 12,000-foot pass) and into the idyllic alpine village of Junbesi on the morning of the seventh day.

Luckily Jim Wilson was there, and we spent the day checking on the progress of the wood piles for the construction that would take place in the fall. As in the construction of all the Hillary schools, the villagers contributed their labor, lugging building stones and timber to the building site, but we paid the wages of the skilled workers—the stone masons and carpenters. Jim was as surprised to see me as I was to see him: the Peace Corps staff in Kathmandu had indicated to him, without daring to tell me about it, that they planned to ship me home on a medical discharge!

After paying off the skilled workers, we set out for the Dudh Koshi gorge and the village of Chaurikharka, which we reached in two days. Ann Wilson and the rest of the Sherpa crew met us there, so at long last the Himalayan Schoolhouse Premonsoon Reconnaissance Expedition was united and at full strength. The next day we all continued along the valley, eventually snaking our way up the steep hill that rises from the confluence of the Imja Khola and Bhote Koshi, where the Dudh Koshi begins. The trail seemed unending until finally, in the distance, we saw Namche Bazaar, the Sherpa capital: several horseshoe-shaped tiers of houses pegged onto the hillside amphitheater (Figs. 2–4). It may not be the most idyllic village of Khumbu, but it is the one on all the maps. I had read and dreamed of this moment for so long that I could not restrain myself from racing ahead of the others, old hands who had seen it all before. I strolled around the dusty lanes, excitedly poking my head into this or that house, looking for the Nepali police checkpost, until the rest of the party arrived.

After completing trekking-permit formalities and stopping in at a chang (home-brewed beer) stall, we staggered past a herd of yak grazing on the upper levels of the amphitheater, finally crested the hill, and descended in a late-afternoon swirling mist to the quiet little village of Khunde, nestled under the harsh black crag of Khumbi Yul Lha, home of the local deity. We headed straight for the two-story stone house of our guide and host, Mingma Tsering, the sardar (chief Sherpa or, in this case, mastermind) of the whole Hillary operation. Mingma's house would be my base of operations for the next few months.

Like most Sherpas, Mingma was on the diminutive side—he couldn't have been much over five feet. But as a leader and organizer he towered over us all. Although illiterate, he had a prodigious memory that enabled him to organize logistics and keep track of dozens of men and tons of matériel in several places at once. Had he been born in the United States, he would have become chairman of General Motors—if GM had set up shop high in the Rockies.

At Mingma's house in Khunde, we were at an altitude of about 13,000 feet, but I felt no effects other than excitement and relief at finally reaching my destination. Expeditions normally take about fifteen days to accomplish what I had done in nine days—a slow pace by the standards of unladen Sherpas. But I was nonetheless pleased to have made up so much time after my hospital stay and to be positioned, at last, to contribute something constructive to Hillary's efforts.

I spent a day poking around the two-room school (built in 1961) in the neighboring village of Khumjung and discovered that each morning the students took turns coming early to clean the place and get it ready for the day.[4] This impressed me because in the Hindu areas where I had taught, no students ever helped keep up the school and grounds—that was a job for low-caste employees. Since everyone in the village was a Sherpa, the issue of employing lower-caste menials as janitors didn't arise.

When I visited the Pangboche school, I taught a few classes. The learn-by-rote methods were those used traditionally throughout Nepal. I was staggered to find the first-year students memorizing multiplication tables up to 11, 12, and 13—but with little idea of what they were doing. Later on I observed midyear exams in Pangboche. I found there the same situation as elsewhere in Nepal and India: cheating is officially wrong, but a lot goes on, with only mild disapproval voiced.

Only three of about thirteen children from Phortse were staying at the hostel Sir Edmund had provided in Pangboche, apparently because of difficult economic conditions caused by a bad potato crop the year before. The first school year had just ended, and some parents were planning not to send their children back for a second year because they thought everything—or at least everything worth learning—should be learned in a year.

The Phortse headman, Sun Tenzing, explained that two of the delinquents were his own children; they were absent only temporarily, he explained, to help take yak up to the higher pastures. He said that if Phortse had its own school, the children would attend, but when food is short it is hard for families to feed both themselves at home and children in the Pangboche hostel. I replied that the children would eat the same amount in Pangboche as at home, but he said that at home, with everything thrown into a single pot, there is enough, but that if

you portion out everything to different pots in different places—home, school, high pastures—then there is not enough to go around. I wasn't domestic enough to see why this was true, but everyone vigorously assured me it was, so I could only write off my contrary view as a product of my own naïveté. (The problem was solved a few years later when Hillary built a school in Phortse.)

Our next move was to head up the valley toward Dudh Pokhari, "milk lake," the source of the Dudh Koshi, "milk river," both names referring to the opacity of the glacial silt. This route would give us a chance to look at the northwest ridge of Taweche, which had defeated the 1963 Hillary party, and at the 24,000-foot peaks along the Tibetan border, at the head of the Ngozumpa Glacier—possible climbing objectives for the full-scale expedition that would assemble in the fall.

Figs. 2 and 3.   Houses at one end of the horseshoe-shaped amphitheater that encompasses Namche, in 1950 (*opposite*) and 1988 (*above*). Even in this relatively unchanged section of Namche, some old houses have been torn down and others bought and sold, and new homes have been built. The earlier photograph is by Charles Houston.

In contrast to my pace on the trip in, ours now was leisurely; we took frequent long rests and sunned ourselves. As always, Mingma had arranged for a few porters to carry the bulk of our gear. We saw the giant fluted white wall of Tamserku rising sheer and straight out of Khumjung and, further up the valley, the rock and ice fang of Ama Dablam. We stopped for the night at a summer yak herders' settlement (*yersa*), where the houses are similar to those in the permanent villages but less substantial and smaller. In *yersas,* people share the single story with their yak, whereas in village houses animals stay on the ground

Fig. 4. The hill above Namche, uninhabited until the 1970s, is now a "suburb," the site of Sagarmatha National Park headquarters, police headquarters, the school, trekking agency staging grounds, and lodges.

floor while their owners live upstairs. The *yersa* houses are built amid a network of dry-stone walls about waist high, which pen the yaks. The little settlements are clean, simple, and picturesque. The next day we proceeded up the valley to Dudh Pokhari, the last of a series of three beautiful emerald green glacier-fed lakes. We moved into one of the stone huts of Gokyo, at 15,600 feet far higher than I had ever been before and more than a thousand feet above Mt. Whitney (14,495 feet), the highest point in the contiguous United States.[5]

The day after our arrival at Gokyo Jim and Ann Wilson and I walked around the lake to look at the 19,770-foot peak that rises out of its western shore. Our real purpose was to look at the Ngozumpa peaks, but why not do a little climbing while we were at it? We moved slowly up the glacial talus, then onto the glacier itself. After sinking to our waists in several places in the soft snow, we moved off the glacier and onto the rocky moraine, then up a snowbank in which Jim cut steps. We climbed up a buttress to a snow-and-rock couloir, but the angle became so steep that we would have had to rope up and belay ourselves to continue. It was too far to go and too late in the day, so we contented ourselves with our estimated high point of 18,500 feet, and again I was surprised to feel no effect from the altitude. The snow was too soft to glissade down, so we had to stumble down the talus back to the lake. When we reached the shore of Dudh Pokhari, the wind was making small waves on the beach. The clear, sky blue water, except for its temperature, could have been straight out of the Caribbean.

At one point on the way back down to Khunde we caught up with our porters, who had stopped by a glacial stream for a drink of water. They were in a rambunctious mood, and a woman was throwing water on one of the men. When I asked for a drink, she politely handed me the bowl. After a few sips I pretended I was going to throw it on her, but then, being a proper gentleman, simply handed her the bowl, whereupon she emptied its contents on my head. Sherpa women are far more forward than their counterparts in the lower hills. The children too are cocky, even brazen, while most other Nepali children are coy and bashful.

During the trek up to Gokyo and back down to Khunde I noticed that Mingma would unfailingly chant a catchy tune every morning and evening, even while walking. I couldn't make out the lyrics, but he was so unceasing about it that I couldn't get it out of my head. When I finally asked him about it, he said it was not a song at all but the endless repetition of a Tibetan prayer that is carved in the stone walls that line the trail into all Sherpa villages: "om mani padme hum" (an essentially untranslatable phrase generally rendered as "Hail to the Jewel [i.e., the Buddha] in the Lotus"). He had been mumbling these words over and over so quickly that I could not distinguish them.

I was excited finally to be in Khumbu but also envious that Hillary had been there first—it seemed that he had already done all the exploration and that I had been born too late. There was nothing new left to do. Even the Sherpas had already been studied (Fürer-Haimendorf had thoughtfully provided me with a page-proof copy of his soon-to-be-released *Sherpas of Nepal*). But then I reflected that no one had noted the change and development that were beginning to take place, and I resolved that at least I could reconnoiter that frontier. (Even so I cannot say that I had any notion at the time that I was involved in making high-altitude history, although in retrospect we clearly were.)

Early in June we started the laborious process of cranking up the Namche community to redo their school. (It had been built originally about three years before with money raised by Tenzing Norgay, Hillary's companion on the summit of Everest. Poorly designed, it quickly became dilapidated.) At a town meeting held outdoors in the warm sunlight, with Tibetan rugs spread out for us to sit on, we explained the standard procedure: the villagers would donate the unskilled labor; we would pay the artisans. This was agreed to without dissent. Thinking that was that, we descended to the bridge site on the Bhote Koshi, where we set up our tents beside the violently swift river with its deafening roar.

The path to the bridge over the Imja Khola a short distance above its confluence with the Bhote Koshi inconveniently ascended and then descended several hundred feet of steep hillside. We planned to build a big bridge just downstream from the confluence and then a smaller one just above it, across the Bhote Koshi, to eliminate the climb (Figs. 5 and 6).[6] We spent two days finding, cutting, and stripping trees on the right bank of the Bhote Koshi. We left them to dry where they lay, planning to move them down to the river in the fall, when they would be lighter. Jim and I worked as hard as we could alongside the Sherpas, but never as productively. They have been toughened by years of hard, rugged living at these heights, and even with a more nutritious diet, we cannot keep up with them.

One evening at our bridge camp the Sherpas ate some yak meat of hoary vintage, the mere smell of which made Jim, Ann, and me nauseous. The Sherpas' tolerance for strong odors was not without adaptive significance in the modern world. Mingma explained that when Sherpas went to India and had to ride a third-class train, they would take along some really old Sherpa cheese. This would make everyone in the train give them a wide berth and assure them a seat on the otherwise fully packed train.

Our progress in rebuilding the Namche school was slow during the next few days. The villagers who turned up to work with us were good, but there were not enough of them, and the headman, Pemba Tsering (Fig. 7) was ineffective in rounding up more. We wanted them to tear down what was left of the back wall of the school and excavate behind it so that it could be rebuilt with the drainage ditch it needed. With no way around the wall, rain and snow runoff had pushed against it and partially collapsed it. An equally exasperating problem was that Pemba Tsering and the workers were interested to the point of obsession in the glamorous but Sisyphean project of leveling the hillside for a football (soccer) field but indifferent to the more mundane work of digging the drainage ditch (Figs. 8 and 9). The contemplated field was a project of vast, not to say grandiose, dimensions. Furthermore, if the ball were kicked out of bounds on the downhill side, one might have to descend

Figs. 5 and 6. This temporary bridge enabled us to get back and forth across the Bhote Koshi during construction of the cantilevered bridges here and a few yards downstream over the Dudh Koshi.

Fig. 7. The Namche headman, Pemba Tsering, holds forth at an early public meeting to discuss rebuilding the Namche school. Tea (note the teacups in the foreground) is served to those attending the meeting.

two thousand feet to retrieve it. Namche was never meant to be a football center.

In the end, Mingma's threats rather than my own exhortations produced action. A natural leader of men, firm, intelligent, and responsible, he was always reflecting on what we were doing and suggesting ways of doing it better (Fig. 10). When he had to make a decision, his concentration would produce such an intimidating scowl on his face that few of us, Sherpas or sahebs (a term used to refer to any high-ranking person, Asian or otherwise), would dare to doubt his judgment. Mingma never hesitated to state his own opinion, but if we did disagree, he followed our decision as if it were his own.

Often he showed more sense than we did. Once during the fall expedition when we were all drinking liberal amounts of chang and *rakshi* (distilled chang) after supper, Mingma, who could, and frequently did, put away as much as any of us, suddenly and unilaterally announced that that was the end of the drinking for the day. He answered our chorus of protestations with the matter-of-fact pronouncement that tomorrow was a big workday and we wouldn't accomplish what we needed to accomplish if we didn't go to bed sober. He simply stated a

Fig. 8. The children of Namche were enthusiastic about the building of the school and helped to carry stones.

self-evident fact, a nonnegotiable demand, and that was the end of the matter.

The Sherpas' confusion of the two Jims, Wilson and Fisher, was solved by my becoming Maachha (fish) Saheb and Jim Wilson's being Jim Saheb. Sherpas who made the distinction between Sherpa and saheb in the 1960s increasingly came to speak of a distinction between Sherpa and Member (of an expedition) by the late 1980s, when the "saheb" suffix was generally dropped.

Our next move after working on the Namche school was up the Thame Valley to the high pasture settlement of Lunak, at about 17,000 feet, with its igloo-shaped rock huts for travelers. On the second day

Fig. 9. Other villagers were more interested in leveling the Namche hillside for a soccer field than in building the school.

we reached Jasamba at 18,000 feet, the last camping spot with a permanent rock shelter this side of the Tibetan border (Fig. 11). The following day we went to the top of the Nangpa La, the gentle, almost-19,000-foot snow-covered pass that was one of the original routes of the Sherpas into Khumbu (Fig. 12).

The approach to the Nangpa La consisted of a "trail" (discernible only from yak bones—there comes a time when a yak just can't go any further) with precipitous peaks on either side and nothing before us but the snow of the wide glacier leading to the crest of the pass. When we reached the top, we saw stretched out in front of us mile after arid mile of the rolling purple-brown hills of Tibet—one of the most dramatic vistas I had ever seen. The great forbidden Tibetan plateau, at an average elevation of 16,000 feet, which I had heard and read about for so long, lay before me. I saw a large concrete slab demarcating the Nepal-China border and was amazed that someone had lugged so much dead weight up there. Jim Wilson and I started down the other side, partly to look at the back side of the Ngozumpa peaks, partly for the thrill of going into Tibet. About a mile beyond the border, on the glacier, was the yak caravan (Fig. 13) we had camped with the night before. As I moved further into Tibet, I became increasingly nervous, imagining

Fig. 10.   Sardar Mingma Tsering barking
orders.

Chinese border guards behind every rock. The yak caravan was setting out again, the yak drivers whooping and whistling and the bells on the yaks clanging as the animals struggled in the deep snow, often sinking up to their shoulders. I walked down toward the snow line and climbed a moraine pile for a look beyond. This was as far as I dared go into Tibet—about two miles. There were probably no Chinese within days of the pass, but I was in no mood to take more chances than I already had, and I could imagine the delight with which a Chinese border patrol would find an American, a member of the Peace Corps at that, on the Tibetan side of the border. I did not relish rotting away in a Chinese prison. (I made my foray on the eve of the Cultural Revolution, five years before Kissinger's secret mission to Beijing.)

I had hoped to try climbing an almost 20,000-foot peak on the border, since I still felt no altitude effects, but it was late in the day to try a peak of that size, and I was loath to leave a fresh set of tracks there that

Fig. 11. Travelers crossing the Nangpa La stay in crude huts like this one at Jasamba (more accurately, this shelter *is* Jasamba), built or commissioned by individuals to accumulate merit.

could torpedo the entire fall expedition if the Chinese discovered them. Therefore I started reluctantly back down into Nepal, away from the sight of the magnificent high, windswept Tibetan plateau.

After enjoying the annual Khumjung-Khunde *Dumje* (a community religious festival with the social atmosphere of a nonstop carnival), Pemba Tharkay, a Phortse man with the strength of an ox, Jim Wilson, and I set off to reconnoiter the back side of the Tamserku ridge. We descended the Dudh Koshi to Monjo before turning up the Kyanshar Khola on a long grueling climb of some five thousand feet. We finally reached a temporary rock shelter about six o'clock, having climbed most of the day in rain. After a supper of *thukpa* (a noodle-based stew) we settled down to a rain-soaked night. I put up my umbrella to shelter my head, but the rest of me got fairly wet. The next morning I woke up early with a rotten cold that, added to lack of sleep, left me feeling quite weak, and I lagged behind Jim, typically tireless, who moved up further and decided that Tamserku's southern col could be approached more favorably from the other side.

From Tamserku we continued down the Dudh Koshi to tackle the next project on our list. We wanted to build an airstrip somewhere near

Fig. 12. The Nangpa La, at almost 19,000 feet, is too high for any beast of burden except the yak.

Lukla, a hamlet of about a half dozen scruffy houses located high above the Dudh Koshi one day's walk below Namche. My journal for the next few days reads as follows:

June 27: At Lukla we took pictures of the airstrip site we are proposing as an alternative to the site down by the Dudh Koshi, which Ed [Hillary] had originally wanted. We think it is inferior to the Lukla location, partly because of the amount of fill-in that would be necessary, partly because of its treacherous crosswind, which is one of Ed's chief concerns. The only problem at Lukla is length; if His Majesty's Government insists on four hundred meters, we will have to buy some farmland. The land is there, and we found that the owners are willing to sell, so in addition to my other responsibilities I have now become the expedition's real estate agent.

June 28: We set off straight up the hill across the river from Lukla for Ghat and a climb of about five thousand feet. It rained most of the day, my cold was worse, and when we stopped at a small *yersa* we were not sure how far we would have to go the next morning to see the col and ridge of Karyolang (another possible objective for the fall expedition).

June 29: The bright and clear morning told us we were lucky, and we could see virtually everything we wanted from the comfort of our sleeping bags inside the tent. We thought this would be a short day, but it involved a climb that ended in a rocky, snow-covered, fairly steep 17,000-foot pass. We de-

Fig. 13.   A yak caravan pauses close to the pass.

scended from the pass and eventually found ourselves on the old high-level route to Khumbu from Junbesi. Again, a good part of the day was spent in rain and mist, and our shoes and socks were soaked.

June 30:   Today was also supposed to be a short day and was for everyone but me. An hour from Tonga we stopped at a yak herder's hut, managed by three young girls who sold us delicious curd and milk for breakfast. From there it was only three hours to our destination of Dudh Kunde, but as I was still feeling weak from my cold, I lagged behind the others, took a wrong turn, and ended up going in the wrong direction down a muddy yak trail. Finally a Sherpa coming my way turned me in the right direction, and I started back up the Solu Khola, reaching camp in an exhausted state about three hours after the others had arrived.

From this point Jim and Ann descended to Junbesi and back to Kathmandu and Banaras, while Mingma, Pemba Tharkay, and I, together with Mingma's newly purchased *dzom* (a yak-cattle crossbreed), returned to Khumbu. We stopped again for breakfast at the hut of the three girls. This time, because I was the only saheb around, the Sherpas were considerably less restrained and joked bawdily back and forth with the girls who lived there. One girl asked if I was married; I said no and asked where I could find a wife around here. Mingma asked me which one I liked, and I said I liked them all, adding that this was a nice place—the food was sweet and so were those who prepared it (the wordplay is funnier in Nepali than in English). The girls laughed at all this, easily as adept at verbal jousting as we were.

After our entertaining breakfast we alternately climbed and descended thousands of feet across a series of north–south spine ridges until we finally dropped down to the by-now-familiar Dudh Koshi. Fortunately Mingma's *dzom* was considerably more tired at the end of the day than at the beginning, and its slower pace not only slowed down the Sherpas but also helped me to keep up and sometimes even get ahead of them with ease. The day of rest and recuperation at Dudh Kunde had restored my strength.

We could have reached Khunde again in a day, but we stopped to wash (Mingma insisted I was getting intolerably dirty) and to see the weekly bazaar at Ghat, which turned out to be nothing more than a merchant with a Japanese rope ladder, a pair of climbing boots from the 1963 American Everest Expedition, and some Chinese cloth and a Tibetan woman who had recently crossed the Nangpa La with a pair of Chinese tennis shoes to sell.

Our travels in Solu-Khumbu depended on Sherpa hospitality. When we arrived at a village where we wanted to spend the night, we would yell up at the window of any convenient house and ask to spend the night there. Permission was inevitably given, whereupon we went upstairs to the main room, cooked our meal on the family fire, and went to sleep on whatever flat surface was available, usually the wood floor. The host typically gave us any extra pillows lying about. We paid for food but, from Junbesi east, not for firewood.

In all our moving about Khumbu, often going our separate ways for days at a time to do different jobs, we never found it hard to keep track of each other. As virtually the only foreigners in Solu-Khumbu all spring and summer, we were so conspicuous that one of us could easily discover where the others were. For the rest of the summer I lived alone with Mingma's family (Figs. 14–18), which I described in my diary:

July 9:   I am living at Mingma's house now, on a foam rubber mattress at the far end of the big room which is, as in most Sherpa houses, the only room (a few wealthy houses also have a private chapel). The eldest member of the household is Mingma's mother, who is about sixty-two. She is a Tibetan who emigrated here from Tibet when she was about twenty. Mingma's father has since married another Tibetan and lives in another house in Khunde, but Mingma's mother stays with her son in their original house. She spends the

Fig. 14. Mingma's son Temba.

whole day spinning woolen thread by hand or, when she's not doing that, keeping her hands busy twirling her prayer wheel in her right hand and counting her rosary beads with her left hand. All rosaries contain 108 beads plus counter beads, which keep track of how many times the circle has been completed. But whatever she is doing with her hands, she rarely ceases praying from the moment she wakes up until the moment she falls asleep. The chant is usually one short phrase—"om mani padme hungri" ["hungri" rather than the more usual "hum" indicates an association with the deity Avolakitesvara, or "glancing eye"]—repeated over and over in a sort of mumbled singsong way. The incessant monotonous droning reminds me of Muzak. It is astonishing how she keeps it up all day without stopping except when she pauses to talk to someone, and even then she continues mumbling her prayer while she listens to the other person's response. But in all this she is quite typical, especially of older people.

Fig. 15.   Mingma's oldest son, Phu Tashi, at fifteen.

Then there are Mingma and his wife, a rather small woman named Ang Doli. She apparently has not been in robust health recently, and the German doctor accompanying a two-man limnological expedition is giving her vitamin injections. She also probably suffers from iodine deficiency (though she has no goiter), which might explain why she has had only one completely normal child out of seven. Four of her children died at or near birth; of three surviving sons one is a cretin, one is profoundly deaf and therefore also dumb, and one is normal.

The cretin is mentally about two years old and physically about six, though he is actually fifteen. He can follow simple commands but cannot talk; he can walk in an awkward, staggering sort of way but falls down often. He has a happy disposition and never cries. He is more or less ignored by the others, simply because it's difficult to establish any sort of relation with him, but he is not ill-treated. In practice his grandmother usually looks after him,

Figs. 16 and 17.   The Khunde house of Sardar Mingma Tsering, in 1964 (*top of page*) and 1988. As the year-round sardar of Sir Edmund Hillary, Mingma has earned enough to enlarge his house. Whereas the house in 1964 had three windows and two doors, by 1988 it had five windows and three doors and two metal-roofed guest rooms. The house now has a private chapel in one end. To make the cooking and eating area easier to heat, it is now closed off from the large room that constitutes the bulk of the house. In the foreground of the 1964 house, Ang Rita, Mingma and Ang Doli's son, observes Sir Edmund beginning to set up a tent.

Fig. 18. Twenty-four years later Ang Rita, who graduated from high school and went to New Zealand to study national parks and recreation, sits at his desk in the National Parks office in Kathmandu.

and a symbiotic relationship has evolved between them: she sees that he's dressed, wipes his nose, and so on, while he brings her things, such as her prayer wheel, if they are out of her reach. [A few years later he and his grandmother died. In retrospect, I would describe the way Sherpas and other Nepalese deal with mentally retarded people as a kind of "mainstreaming." They are not singled out for special treatment, good or bad, but are simply accepted in the family and community for what they are.]

After him comes Temba, who is almost totally deaf and who has therefore not learned to speak. He seems quite bright and can usually get his point across in sign language. He is a sweet kid but a little short on self-confidence because he cannot hear. He is about ten years old. [After the Khunde Hospital was built in 1966, he was fitted for a hearing aid but was able to get no practical use out of it. Despite his considerable artistic talent and financial success as a painter, he had not married as of 1988, when he was in his early thirties. Sherpas matter-of-factly point to his inability to speak as the reason for his remaining a bachelor.]

Then there is the very cute, roly-poly five-year-old, Ang Rita, who is completely normal and the apple of everyone's eye. His sunny disposition lights up the whole house. [After the iodine injections Ang Doli eventually gave birth to another son, who in 1989 was attending college in Kathmandu.]

Finally there are the three *dzom* that live downstairs and the aged Tibetan mastiff that lives in a doghouse outside the front door. It seems like a strange household in some ways, but it is very enjoyable and interesting to live here, and I've grown fond of them all. Sherpa family life is much more akin to American family life than Nepalese Hindu family life; that is, women are much more equal and assertive, children are not so shy, and of course Sherpa hospitality is unrivaled.

One night Mingma's cat killed its second chicken of the week, and something had to be done. At first Mingma thought of killing it, or at least having it killed, but then decided the problem could be solved by simply knocking its teeth out, thus sparing the cat's life and avoiding sin on Mingma's part. So Pemba Tharkay held the cat while Mingma bashed its teeth out with the dull side of a steel meat cleaver. The scene sent shivers down my spine, but the Sherpas seemed unaffected. I would have found it easier to kill it. Thus was sown a small seed of skepticism about the compassion of Buddhism (or at least a knowledge of its limits) and the status of Khumbu as Shangri-La.

In the meantime I discovered that I had roundworms, among other unwelcome intestinal visitors, and the nearest medicine was with the German limnological expedition up at Tsola Tso, a large glacial lake beside Khumbu Glacier. So Mingma and I, with Mingma's brother-in-law, Ang Pemma, as porter, set out for Pangboche, then Tsola Tso, and finally Everest base camp.

We turned up toward Khumbu Glacier, past the summer settlements of Pheriche and Phulung Karpo on a meadow carpeted with alpine flowers, then on up the moraine to the lake of Tsola Tso and the German scientific expedition. Having lived entirely on rice and potatoes for several months, I was delighted when the two German scientists insisted we stay for lunch and eventually dinner, since they ate almost entirely out of cans and had delicacies I had not tasted for more than two years. The next day we headed for Lobuche, a collection of two or three empty rock huts, where we made a fire to dry out after the morning's constant rain. We camped at a tiny pond called Gorak Shep. The next morning Ang Pemma and I threaded our way past and around the seracs and streams in the glacier until we reached the American base camp at about 17,500 feet, near the foot of the icefall.

It was all there: in a blinding arc stood the white flank of Nuptse, the great Lhotse face, the west ridge of Everest, the Lho La, and the shining silver ridge of Pumori. Ang Pemma knew the icefall only too well: he had been in the middle of it scarcely a year before (during the 1963 American Mount Everest Expedition) when Jake Breitenbach was crushed under a serac the size of a freight car (a rock inscription in Gorak Shep commemorates his death). Ang Pemma was half buried himself, unconscious, and in need of several stitches around his right eye. But he was back ferrying loads up the icefall again a week after the accident.

The roundworms sapped my strength, but the going back down was easier, and we went on to Dukla for hot milk and curds. On the way to Dingboche we stopped by a hut where we were offered chang and tea by none other than the infamous Pangboche Pong, a less-than-fastidious kitchen boy from Hillary's last expedition, so named for the unsavory cook in the mountaineering spoof *The Ascent of Rumdoodle*.

We bushwhacked up a hillside until we finally reached Nagarjung, a cave inhabited by a hermit monk, or lama, year-round (Fig. 19). Fürer-Haimendorf called the 15,297-foot cave one of the highest permanently settled habitats in central Asia. When we visited the monk, Gelung Nawang, he was, at eighty-four, a pleasant old man who spent most of his time in prayer and meditation. He lived entirely alone, but people from the villages below ferried up food for him, and it turned out that Pangboche Pong's sister cooked for him. My stomach was still giving me trouble, so the lama gave me some of his "medicine"—for my long life, among other things. Later that night I felt even worse than I had been feeling and vomited several times, a rare occurrence for me. I finally realized that the "medicine"—a marble-sized ball of tsampa (roasted barley flour), ghee, and sugar—was probably at least six months old and also contained some of the lama's urine. It may have helped give the lama long life, but it nearly ended mine.

During those days in higher places I lived frequently on tea and tsampa, which was added to the tea to make a hot, stimulating, and nourishing paste. Barley was not approved for trade to Nepal by the Chinese, but apparently quite a bit of it ended up in Khumbu anyway. I asked Mingma what Sherpas thought of the Chinese, and his answer was interesting: he said the Chinese claim all men should work equally, including the rich, and that this was fine with the Sherpas. But he didn't like the eviction of the lamas from the monasteries, because he thought the lamas had a useful function apart from work and that they should be allowed to pursue it in the monasteries. He added that the worst thing about the coming of the Chinese to Nepal would be that there would then be no more expeditions and hence no more jobs for Sherpas.

In the Thame Valley I visited a newly built *gompa* (Buddhist temple or monastery) at Thamo, populated by refugee monks and nuns from Tibet. There Kappa Kalden (see Plates 14–16), the most famous painter of Khumbu, was painting delicate, detailed frescoes on the walls in a

Fig. 19. Gelung Nawang, the hermit of Nagarjung, in his cave above Ding-boche, where he receives and ministers to anyone who calls on him.

fascinating process that was both cooperative and didactic: he traced the pictures in charcoal; his son followed behind, filling in the outlines with the paint. The paintings, whether on *gompa* and chapel walls or on rolled scrolls called *thankas,* are an integral part of Tibetan Buddhism. With the virtual elimination of this art in Tibet under the Chinese, it was a rare chance to see the skill being practiced and passed on to the next generation.

I spent most of the rest of the summer commuting daily to Namche to try to keep the school-building project on track. Often no one showed up to work, or those who did sweated away on the cursed football field, a project that intrigued them much more than the pedestrian school. Although I threatened, lectured, and cajoled, I was always limited by my lack of Sherpa language. With Mingma's aid, however, most of the work eventually got done. My ultimate threat was that Sir Edmund had had many requests for village schools, and if Namche wasn't prepared to build one, plenty of other villages were eager to take their place in the queue.

Progress was so slow that toward the end of July I decided the best thing to do for Namche would be to plow it over. The day after one exhortatory meeting only one worker showed up. The headman, Pemba Tsering, said he was willing to donate several hundred rupees to pay poorer people to bring up wood but that no other rich man would donate anything. Taking this as a suggestion that we should pay for hauling wood, I said that the school was for Namche, not for us, and we weren't willing to pay anything for unskilled labor. Finally Pemba Tsering said that if no one else was interested, there was nothing further he could do, and he would not blame us for abandoning the project. I hadn't anticipated that response but rallied by pointing out that we had already invested considerable time, trouble, and expense, and if the villagers did not want the school, I expected them to reimburse us for some of our costs, such as the stonemasons' fees. He in turn had not anticipated this rejoinder, but I stood my ground. Finally we decided that the next day there would be one last general meeting at which the villagers could decide whether they wanted the school or not.

No one showed up for the 11:00 A.M. meeting. The checkpost commander, Captain Lama (the first Sherpa to hold that position at the Namche police post) explained that part of the problem with the Namche school was that many of the rich people send their children to Darjeeling schools and that the community is divided into factions. Still, I did not believe the villagers could be so shortsighted as to give up this opportunity of a lifetime—Darjeeling schools and factions notwithstanding—so I decided to visit once more some of the influential men to be sure they understood the implications of not following through on their original commitment. Gradually I gathered together a few reluctant souls, who said they had not come to the meeting because no one else had—a good example of their level of leadership. This time they all agreed to carry up the wood, almost as if they had not known it was there. I said I had heard that before, and I needed to have an ironclad commitment; they promised to have all the wood brought up from the river within five days. To my astonishment, they did. By common consent each household that did not furnish a worker was to be fined six rupees.

The one big job left for me during this monsoon reconnaissance was to finalize arrangements for the airstrip at Lukla. We decided to go ahead with the Lukla site instead of the one down by the river, but I had to measure the land, photograph it in detail, buy it, and make sure the necessary paperwork was done to make it legally ours—or, rather, His Majesty's Government's. Mingma and I and the owners measured the land with a rope, bargained over the price, signed the contracts, and bought ten rupees' worth of chang to celebrate the closing of this real estate deal. We purchased a strip of land about 1,200 feet long from five landowners for Rs 6,350 (about $835).[7] We proudly thought we had the makings of a respectable airstrip, but the civil aviation advisor later granted, and then only grudgingly, that it looked "fine for an irregularly used 'emergency-style' strip."

With the Lukla real estate deal concluded, I turned my attention toward getting back to Kathmandu to meet Ed Hillary and the expedition members who would be arriving in September. Phurba Tenzing and I said good-bye to Mingma Tsering and set off for the long walk down the valley to Dharan in the eastern Tarai.

We stopped at Takshindu Monastery in Solu but were kept awake by an incongruously noisy party of lamas and nuns. Phurba Tenzing too had been sick in Khumbu, and the lama doctor who treated him told him the problem was that I had offended a god when I went for a swim in the Sun Koshi on the march in. The cure was to drink plenty of milk, a prescription I preferred over lama's urine and one that had the not insignificant advantage of apparently working. Here and at villages along the way I was repeatedly asked if Sir Edmund would help with a new school. Good news travels fast.

The bridge over the Solu Khola, below Ringmo, had been swept away a few hours before we had planned to cross it. Downstream, however, we found a narrow spot and, fortuitously, a plank nearby that enabled us to get across and thus avoid the half day's delay the detour would otherwise have cost us.

As I had received no mail since leaving Kathmandu several months before, I was curious to check out the rumor that a packet addressed to me had been sent in care of the school inspector in the Solu-Khumbu district capital of Saleri. When I reached Saleri, the inspector was away with other officials, examining the washed-out bridge site, so I asked an office worker (a *pyun* in Nepali, in a borrowing from the English word *peon*) if he knew anything about my mail. He said if it were there, it would probably be locked up in a closet. It began to look as if I would not receive it since I could not wait for the inspector to return. As a last resort I started looking around the office and tugging on closet doors, much to the dismay of the *pyun*, who seemed worried that I would discover top-secret documents in his care. On top of one closet I noticed a thick brown envelope and decided to have a look, although the *pyun* was by this time quite frantic. I pulled down the envelope, blew off an accumulation of dust, and found my name written underneath.

Thus after months without any mail, I finally received letters and news of the outside world. As I read through the contents of the envelope, I enjoyed the strange sensation of reading in August letters written in May—among them a long-awaited one from Ed Hillary. Fortunately we had second-guessed each other pretty well, and I had done all that he had asked. Another letter, from the University of Chicago, rather sternly advised me to enroll there the following month, noting that the Himalayas would wait for me. I ignored the advice.

I stayed the night with the hospitable Swiss couple who ran the Tibetan refugee camp at Chalsa and was served the best meal I had eaten in months. (My hosts commented at dinner on the strangely named new singing group the Beatles. This was the first time I had heard of them, and I was confused, understanding the comment on the Beatles to refer to the particular beetle I had just noticed in my rice.) The next day we crossed the Solu Khola en route to the out-of-the-way village of Nechhe. My only reason for going there was to talk to last year's Chaurikharka teacher, whom Ed had liked, to see if he would return.

The long uphill route was uncomfortable in the summer heat, but more disturbing was our difficulty finding a place to eat. The people in the first house we stopped at told us that they were Chhetris, and therefore we could not cook on their kitchen fire. After months of generous and unrestrained hospitality in the homes of the Sherpas, who had no apparent caste or food restrictions, this refusal was a shock, especially since we were suffering from the heat and were famished as well. When we finally arrived in the village, we found the school closed for vacation and the teacher gone. The next day we did bump into the Namche teacher on the trail to Okhaldhunga; he wanted Rs 200 per month (about $26), and I told him that Ed would meet his demand.

As we proceeded south to Diktel and Bhojpur, we were constantly asked the questions one meets on the trail: where were we going, where were we coming from, and why? The repeated queries became irksome, especially when we were hot and hungry and asking in the first place if we could eat, only to be answered with more questions. So Phurba Tenzing took to giving facetious responses: asked where we live, he answered, "In a house" (which is much funnier in Nepali than in English). Asked who he was, Phurba Tenzing once replied that his father was a Sherpa and his mother a Brahman (again the phrasing loses something in translation but is hilarious in Nepali because it is an outrageous and impossible genealogy).

When we reached Dhankuta, a large Newar bazaar a day's walk from the Tarai, a giant Russian helicopter landed on the parade ground. The Russian crew was training a Nepali pilot from Dhankuta, who was just dropping in for an hour to see his family. The Russian crew, one of whom spoke English, gave us a complete tour of the chopper. I was struck by our having more in common with each other than we did with the Nepalis, although we were supposed to be deadly enemies. For example, we talked to each other as we pushed our way past the mob of villagers, who peered into the chopper from outside while we sat inside—small matters, but they indicated our basic educational and technological similarity. The pilot disconcertingly described everything in military terms. When I asked him how many passengers the chopper could hold, he answered, "Forty-five men, fully armed."

In Dhankuta I paid Phurba Tenzing and went on to Dharan alone. I carried my own load and camped near Mulghat by the river, where I built a fire and cooked my own *dal-bhat* (lentils and rice) for a change. The service of a Sherpa is so comprehensive that one tends to do nothing but walk and sit, and it was refreshing to be more directly engaged in the actual processes of daily life.

I started for Dharan at 4:00 A.M., to escape the terrible heat of the day. It was pleasant walking by the light of the full moon, but soon it was dawn and the sun caught me going up the last long hill. A friendly Brahman from Taplejung had just finished cooking his food and offered me some, which saved me the time and bother of cooking for myself. Then I moved on up the trail with my rucksack, which weighed a little over 50 pounds. I became convinced that the real unsung heroes of Nepal are the midland porters, the tough men who carry between 80 and 120 pounds up to the hill villages and bazaars for very little pay. Finally I reached the top of the last hill I would have to climb for a few weeks. The pass was shrouded in mist, but a short way down the other side I broke through the cloud cover and there, after so many weeks and months of endless up and down, was the great Gangetic plain of

India in all its unlimited and unrestrained flatness. In its own way, the view was as arresting as that from the Nangpa La into Tibet a few weeks earlier.

In Dhankuta I had had to decide whether to go on to Dharan or proceed on a tack east to Sikkim. Hope Cook, the maharani of Sikkim, had written, asking me to stay in the palace when I arrived there after crossing the Nepalese border, which she assured me I would have no trouble doing. After explaining the difficulties of obtaining the permits necessary to come via India, she wrote: "We were intrigued by the possibility of your entering from Nepal, as it can be done—although I think that as far as Westerners are concerned you would be a pioneer." My boots, however, had given their all, having taken me some six hundred miles, and I had little time, energy, or money left. I was also tempted to see more of the Tarai, but there were just too many tasks to attend to in Kathmandu before Ed and the other expedition members arrived. So I turned my eyes westward and flew to Kathmandu from Biratnagar.

At the Kathmandu airport I ran into Willie Unsoeld, once again my Peace Corps boss after his year's hiatus recuperating in the States from frostbite. I had had as much trouble sending as receiving mail; he had lost all track of me and said he had planned to give me three more days before sending out search parties. I also saw the American ambassador, Henry Stebbins, at the airport. He had read a copy of a long report I had sent to Ed from Khunde and said he thought it was a penetrating analysis.

My job for the first two weeks of September was to take care of the myriad details that Ed wanted resolved before his arrival. At the top of the list was obtaining permission to build the Lukla airstrip—the biggest question mark in our whole plan. I had dinner one evening with a woman whose husband had recently skipped across the border into Tibet, photographed a Khamba raid on a Chinese supply train, and brought the movies back across the border; they had been shown on British television, causing a great uproar in Singha Durbar (the man, whose name was Patterson, was jailed for ten days before being evicted from the country). Subsequently, His Majesty's Government began cracking down on all expeditions, and permission to build the Lukla airstrip was jeopardized. Mr. Shah at the foreign office said he was very pleased with what he called the very thorough documents on the airstrip that I had sent him by runner. But he said in effect that permission to go ahead was too sensitive a matter for him or me to handle, and it would have to await a conference between Ed and the ministers involved.

My journal entries record the frenetic pace:

September 9: I rented a jeep and went to meet Mingma, as per the schedule we made over a month ago, at the Unsoeld's house, where we picked up all the expedition gear we had stored there. We set up our biggest tent on the grounds of the British embassy for temporary storage, then raced to the airport to meet Ed's plane from Delhi. As we half expected, it had been turned back by bad weather in the Simra pass.

This evening I hosted a big feast at the Unsoeld's. My complete Sherpa costume, including Tibetan quartz sunglasses, was a great hit. All our expedition Sherpas attended, plus some of the Solu aristocracy, Sardar Ang Tharkay, who had been on Everest about six times and was sardar for the French on Annapurna [in 1950; this was the first ascent of an 8,000-meter peak], and of course our hosts, Willie and Jolene Unsoeld. In her usual selfless, hospitable way Jolene had done most of the food planning and preparation, and I was left with the relatively minor job of paying. After dinner Willie showed slides of his Everest traverse, which fascinated all of us, especially the Sherpas. The only person missing was Ed, whose plane had been diverted to Banaras.

September 10: Mingma and I drove to the airport on the off chance that Ed's plane would come in today. He had not arrived, but Mingma spied Peter Mulgrew standing on the runway beside a great pile of crates and enormous burlap sacks. Peter had lost both legs below the knees after collapsing near the summit of Makalu in 1961, but he walked so skillfully, without even a cane, that on level ground one could not detect that he had artificial limbs. The rest of the day I spent shuttling between Singha Durbar and the airport, getting various stamps placed on assorted sheets of paper. By the time we finished with red tape, it was too late to actually start checking gear through customs, so we asked a couple of Sherpas to guard it for the night. Meanwhile Ed had finally come in from Banaras, and the expedition finally seemed officially under way.

This evening Charles Wylie invited Peter and Ed and me for dinner. During drinks beforehand one Micky Weatherall, now doing road construction work here, stopped by; he claimed to have been on Everest in 1924 with Mallory and Irvine. I was startled and later remarked to Ed that he must have been extremely young then; Ed replied that I should take anything he says with a grain of salt. Micky had been with the 1924 expedition, but I later discovered that he disliked Mallory, one of Ed's all-time heroes. Various visitors appear at our camp in the British embassy grounds, including Jimmy Roberts, who had a long argument with Ed about the correct altitude of various locations in Khumbu. There is no agreement, for example, even about the height of Namche, and guesses range from 10,000 to 12,800 feet, with the general consensus closer to 12,000.

September 11: Ed and Charles Wylie and I went to do battle in Singha Durbar over the airstrip and radio. The Foreign Ministry needed to know the radio frequencies we planned to use and referred us to the Communications Department. Later in the day, our radio expert, Peter Mulgrew, and I got a rather cool, bordering on rude, reception from the Communications Department official, who apparently was annoyed that he had received nothing in writing from the Foreign Office. I had begun to boil over when Peter's cooler head prevailed and he smoothed things out. The plan of attack now is to write a letter specifying our frequencies to the Foreign Office and asking them to clear them with the Communications Department. In the meantime I was back at the airport periodically, seeing to the loading of the truck I had rented; we needed two trips with the truck and about three additional jeep loads to get all the gear to the embassy camp. In the evening we were all invited to dinner at the home of the British ambassador, Tony Duff. I had been rushing about at such a mad pace the whole day that I didn't even meet the other expedition members until the dinner.[8]

September 12:   Another mad day taking care of myriad exasperating details, with the usual difficulties compounded by the fact that many of the stores are shut because of the Saturday holiday. Still no word on permission to build the Lukla airstrip. We had our first meals at the embassy camp; Ang Pemma does a good job but only wiped the tomatoes off with a towel—I can see that one of my main jobs will be to keep a sanitary kitchen so that everyone stays healthy.

September 13:   While the others were sorting the gear into sixty-pound loads, I continued handling local problems: buying, ordering, bargaining, finagling, wheeling and dealing. Most of the latter activities involve Ed, and I serve more or less as a local guide, seeing him safely in and out of the labyrinthine corridors of Singha Durbar. In the afternoon a few of us took the "mountain goat"—a rough-terrain motorbike we hoped Peter Mulgrew would be able to ride—to the Swayambunath hill for a trial run. On the parts that I thought approximated the trail to Khumbu, the performance was disappointing; on the rocky, steep sections, riding it would require such agility, concentration, and strength that Mulgrew would find it easier to walk than to ride.

   After dinner we had a whopping good film show at Charles Wylie's: his movie of the 1957 Macchapuchhare expedition [Macchapuchhare is the Matterhorn-shaped peak that towers over Pokhara, in western Nepal] and the excellent film of the 1963 Schoolhouse Expedition.[9]

September 14:   A typical day. To Singha Durbar with Mulgrew to check on radio frequencies, before that to USAID to get the expedition movie tripod fixed, to Shanta Bhawan Hospital to see if we could get any battery acid (we could not), to Mercantile Corp. to pick up a good piece of window glass (they did not have it yet), to the bazaar in Asan to pick up the twenty pounds of six-inch nails we had decided to get since we could not get eight-inch nails without having them custom made (they were not ready), to another shop for a pound of one-inch nails for nailing up crates, to a store to get three biscuit tins for transporting cement, back to USAID for health posters for the schools, and so forth. One pleasant break in the day came when I had lunch with Harry and Betsy Barnes. Harry is number two at the American embassy [he later served as ambassador to Rumania, India, and Chile]. Harry becomes fluent in the language of every country to which he is assigned and to my chagrin speaks better Nepali than any of us.

This evening there was another film show for us and resident British subjects at the British ambassador's house. After everyone else had left, the expedition members sat around with the ambassador and his family and had one for the road. I was entranced as Ed dominated the conversation with his tales of practical joking in the Antarctic. His stories were hilarious, with Peter Mulgrew adding his own humorous version from time to time. New Zealanders seem to be a relaxed and happy-go-lucky lot. Of course as the only Yank I take plenty of ribbing, but so far I think I have given about as good as I have gotten.

September 15: Filed the last required radio information and turned in Mingma's passport application (so he can visit New Zealand at the end of the expedition) at Singha Durbar. Despite the pouring rain, Jim Wilson's plane arrived on schedule from Banaras. Unfortunately the rest of the freight has still not arrived from Calcutta. Our camp has become a swamp now—I hope the British ambassador does not mind. The expedition members and a few guests went to Boris's apartment for a late party—drinks from about ten to midnight, then dinner in the palatial hotel dining room. [Boris Lissanevitch was a former ballet dancer who had fled to Paris after the Bolshevik revolution and later opened a nightclub in Calcutta, where he met King Tribhuvan. The king invited him to open a hotel after the 1950 revolution. Boris's Royal Hotel, a partially renovated Rana palace, was virtually the only hotel then in Kathmandu. Boris was famous for, among other things, his lavish hospitality. He died in 1985.] It was all a little much for me since I was feeling the effects of four different inoculations I had gotten earlier in the day.

September 16: We were all pretty groggy at breakfast. Ed and I went to the USAID office at Rabi Bhawan to see about chartering their chopper to fly Mulgrew to Lukla (since the "mountain goat" will not work out for him) and then had a lunch that included sausages and canned peaches. After my normal Nepali diet, I find it incongruous to be eating so well in Nepal; what I eat with the expedition I otherwise eat only at the houses of American officials with commissary privileges.

September 17: Up till three in the morning catching up on correspondence, then up again at six and to the embassy for breakfast and breaking camp. The three trucks arrived on schedule at seven, and by about half past eight we were loaded up and under way. The convoy moved off, some of us in jeeps of friends and well-wishers who came along to watch the show, some on the tops of trucks. I cleared us through the Sanga checkpost easily, then on to Banepa with only minor hitches, such as boiling radiators. The trucks could not handle the hill up to the hospital, so porter loads were carried up and set out in lines to be distributed to the porters. The only problem was to get the coolies to take the odd-shaped loads, such as sections of metal roofing; these weigh the same as the crates and boxes but are much clumsier to carry.

The approach march consists of nine members [Ed, Jim Wilson, Mingma, and Lyn Crawford were to fly on to Jiri to begin the construction of the Junbesi school], six Sherpas, and 231 coolies [or porters; I use the terms interchangeably, though Sherpas say "coolie" where we would say "porter"], with myself as leader and Tenzing Ngenda, a young and inexperienced but highly competent Sherpa, as my sardar. [He was killed a few years later in a mountaineering accident.] It's all a little heady: less than a year ago merely being on an expedition was a dream, and now here I am, appointed by Sir Edmund Hillary to lead his expedition's approach march.

In the spring and summer I was so overwhelmed by the cleanliness of Khumbu that I resolved to try to make our fall expedition as litter free as possible. I wanted somehow to convince our 231 porters plus Sherpas and members not to throw paper or rubbish on the trail but instead to save it and burn it at the evening's camp. Unfortunately, I was unable to rally support for this idea. [Years later litter has become a major problem for the whole area.] We descended the long hill to Panchkhal for the night, and it was a great relief to be pounding along the trail again, away from the noise and smells and cares of city life. There was great confusion the first night as we searched for the items we needed, which were all in different loads, but finally we settled down to a good dinner. It seemed an unnecessary extravagance to have the leader's tent put up just for me, so I shared a tent with Max Pearl, the expedition doctor, whom I assisted as translator at his late-afternoon sick calls. Having had hardly any sleep last night, I plopped down fully clothed onto my sleeping bag and did not move till morning.

September 18:   We were off about half past six and stopped for breakfast near a stream, where we all went swimming. This morning I got the *naikes* (non-Sherpas who take general charge of the porters) to agree to push on to-day to Dumre,[10] on the hill above Dolalghat [Fig. 20]. The other expedition members and I accordingly charged on up the hill in the afternoon, only to be halted by protests from the porters behind and below us. None of my frenzied gesticulations and bellowings had any effect, and I had no choice but to retreat ignominiously back down to the river. The only retaliation open to me was to withhold the porters' cigarette ration for the day. I told them I wanted to cut a day off the number of scheduled days (fourteen) to Lukla, since the marches seem ridiculously short to me, and they said they would try.

September 19:   We climbed up the long, hot Dolalghat hill, and when we reached Chaubas the coolies were not keen to go on because of lack of shelter further down the trail. I certainly did not have tarps for 231 porters, so I was forced to scrap my plan to cut a day off the schedule. The basic problem is that we did not escape from Banepa until mid-afternoon; after that, because of shelter and water requirements for so many people, it becomes impossible to make up time. Our Chaubas camp was a beautiful one, overlooking a grand vista of green hills rolling one after the other all the way to the Indian plain.

September 20:   Today brought us to Reshyang Gompa, where we stored our gear in the *gompa* courtyard. The lama's wife wore a sari, but with a striped,

Fig. 20. A porter carries his load across a chain bridge; the iron links are forged by low-caste blacksmiths (Kāmi) in Those, a village halfway between Kathmandu and Namche Bazaar.

Sherpa-style apron—an interesting Tamang-Sherpa combination not found in Khumbu.

September 21: Today we camped at Chitre. The day's marches seem short— easy enough for me, with only my backpack, to say. But our heavily laden porters come struggling in all afternoon; we are kept busy handing out cigarettes, checking loads, setting up tents, and holding Max's sick call, which attracts many of our porters plus local villagers. The monsoon is in its last gasp—the sun increasingly breaks through the mist and rain.

On a typical day we got off about half past six, had breakfast about nine, then took a brief nap and later on, if a suitable stream presented itself, a swim. We usually got into camp by two and had tea before organizing the porters as they came in. The route on the twenty-second was pleasant—uncharacteristically level or downhill. By our sixth night we had reached Kirantichap. On day seven Max and I detoured to Jiri just as the plane landed with the second load of our gear and the last-but-one member of our expedition, the Indian physiologist Lahiri. (Despite a flurry of telegrams announcing the imminent arrival of the last member of our expedition—the flamboyant, irrepressible, and unpredictable Calcutta journalist Desmond Doig—he never did turn up.) No porters were available to carry the loads, so I sent a Sherpa over to the main trail to hijack ten of our porters, whose loads other coolies would carry on top of their own—these loads would now weigh 120 pounds, twice the normal freight. We also bought 18 pounds of yak cheese in Jiri.

September 25:   A good number of coolies wanted to quit this morning, despite the fact that they had signed on for the whole trip. They had not bothered to find substitutes or to tell us the evening before. We did find a few porters in Those but had to harangue a number of others into continuing. Once I saw that we had enough carrying power, I set off with the money box, followed soon by some of the porters who had quit, in pursuit of their wages. When K.C. [short for Khatri-Chhetri], our teacher for the new school in Junbesi, and I got to the bottom of the long hill, I thought we should pay them all off, but K.C. was adamant and said that since they had caused us so much trouble, they should not be paid until we reached Chiangma, our camp for the night on the other side of the long hill. So off we went up the hill, with the unpaid porters wailing in the distance. About halfway up they again pleaded for their money, and K.C. really put them through the verbal ringer [Figs. 21 and 22]. After reviling and haranguing them, he made them each twist their own ears while going from a standing to a squatting position twenty times before I paid them off, a conventional method for humiliating someone. I thought K.C. was overdoing it, and in retrospect wish I had reined him in.

September 26:   More porter trouble this morning, and we finally left without five loads. I told our tail-end Charlie, Pemba Gyaltzen, to stay with them until we had rounded up some porters, which we did in the villages below Chiangma. I arrived late for breakfast at the foot of the Lamjura-Bhanjyang but had a swim anyway, then up three thousand feet to Seti Gompa, a good camping spot except for the leeches, which we tried to get rid of by pitching them over the bank or, in my case, by incinerating them one by one.

September 27:   I awoke this morning to find blood all over my air mattress— a leech had gotten to me during the night. Poetic justice, said Jim Milledge. I was puzzled as to where I had been bitten and only later realized that the leech had gotten me right on top of the head, where my hair was matted with dried blood. Then up the trail and over the pass to Junbesi, carrying about sixty pounds now, following Willie Unsoeld's advice that the best way to get fit is to carry heavy loads.

September 28:   Yesterday the confusion of sorting loads to stay in Junbesi while the school is being built and loads to go on to Lukla was compounded by the pouring rain; the process had to be done under tarpaulins in the courtyard of Ang Dorje, a wealthy villager. Today the weather was clear, but most of the porters wanted to turn back. Finally we persuaded some to go on by bribing them with cigarettes and got replacements for the others, so that we

Fig. 21.   The approach-march disciplinarian, K.C., applies harsh measures to porters who violated their "contracts" by quitting without giving notice.

had to abandon only ten loads. We deducted one rupee from the pay of those who quit and sent them on their way.

September 29:   Max and I mounted two of Ang Dorje's horses and rode down the valley to the village of Beni. Ed had told the headmen earlier that he would send me down to see the school to decide if and to what extent we should aid it. The ride to Beni was delightful, about one and a half hours on a wide, smooth trail through pine groves. I had not expected a reception, but when I arrived I found hanging on the front wall of the school a big red banner on which were sewn white Nepali letters reading Welcome Mr. Jim Saheb. While Max vaccinated the children, I got data on the school, which has been built without any outside assistance. What they want is a new roof (they lose a lot of class days during the monsoon because the leaks are so bad), glass for their windows, furniture, and teaching aids. They seem to have done about as much as they can on their own, so I am going to recommend that we help them.

Fig. 22.   The approach-march coolies were drawn from diverse groups: groups like Tamangs and Sherpas that speak Tibeto-Burman languages as well as high-caste Hindus like this Brahman or Chhetri man. In 1964 the wages for carrying a sixty-pound load were six rupees (a little less than a dollar) per day.

The Junbesi school was largely finished by the time I arrived (Fig. 23), and I was left the relatively unsatisfying job of haggling over local issues with the villagers. As is typical with larger aid projects everywhere, the physical structures are easy to build; the human problems, however, are difficult to resolve. One issue was whether to enroll those Beni students who live closer to Junbesi than to Beni. More important was the problem of a house for the teacher, K.C. Ed, on his way through a week before, had told the villagers to furnish a house for the teacher. The villagers' interpretation of this instruction had been that they were to provide the house; we were to pay rent for the house—an interpretation I said was completely unacceptable. It took a couple days

Fig. 23. The Junbesi school begins to take shape in the rice fields below the village.

of haggling to convince them that Ed really was not going to pay for the teacher's house and that he was not, after all, an eternal cash register. Once they realized this, they got together and decided to build a new house. After more discussion we realized that the site of the new house, right next to the school, would diminish the area of the playground. After much more discussion the villagers agreed to give a small house rent free for ten years if we would install windows in it.

October 4:   Amid garlands and prayer scarfs, and with K.C. straddling a hole in the still-unfinished floor of the school while delivering a lecture on Saraswati, the Hindu goddess of learning, the Junbesi school was declared officially open. Since all the carpenters were still busy inside, the school moved into the sunshine outside, where K.C. registered the students and distributed books. By the second day about a hundred students were enrolled, of whom about sixty showed up for classes [Figs. 24–26].

October 11:   The school is essentially finished, so we took our leave from Junbesi and headed on up the trail to Takshindu Monastery, and up the Dudh Koshi again to Kharikhola and Puyang. I was startled upon reaching the top of the hill before Lukla to look down at the clear outline of the airstrip. When we arrived we could see that the rough work, at least, was nearly finished. I talked over the radio to Ed upriver at the bridge-building site, and the next day we sauntered past the Chaurikharka school, which is coming along nicely,

Fig. 24. A Junbesi woman brings her children to school the first day.

then raced at breakneck speed to the bridge camp, where I filled in Ed on the approach march and progress at Junbesi.

We all rose fairly early the next morning and climbed two thousand feet up the east side of Kwangde to reconnoiter the route on Tamserku, which looks difficult but not impossible. A more or less informal race developed, and I was pleased to be able to keep up with the leaders. Peter Farrell and Jim Wilson went on to establish base camp on Tamserku while the rest of us returned to Lukla to finish the airstrip and the Chaurikharka school.

During this phase of the expedition a number of far-flung projects were going on at once: some of us worked on the Lukla airstrip, some on the Chaurikharka school, others at the bridge site or on the mountain or at the Namche school. All of this work was organized with the utmost skill by the indefatigable Mingma Tsering. Unable to make or take notes or even read, he nevertheless kept the myriad details—which operation needed what kinds of equipment and food—all in his head, and he never missed a trick.

October 19: Today the incomparable Swiss pilot, Emile Wick, made a dramatic flight over the airstrip and dropped our mail. He came in at 13,000 feet,

Fig. 25. K.C., the Junbesi teacher, enrolls prospective students.

Fig. 26. Two students learn their KaKhaGas (the Nepali equivalent of the ABCs), sitting in the midst of wood chips as the carpenters finish their work.

Fig. 27. On the ninth day of Dasain (the biggest Hindu festival of the year), Hindus sacrifice animals to protect their vehicles against accidents. At the airport in Kathmandu, a goat is about to be sacrificed in front of a twin-otter aircraft bound for Lukla. Its blood was smeared on the image of the Hindu deity Bhairab painted on the side of the plane; Bhairab is associated, inappropriately it would seem in an aircraft, with destruction.

then continued circling lower and lower until he swooped right over the field. I hope he liked what he saw; otherwise we have put in a great deal of work for nothing.

I was relieved, during the next morning's scheduled radio broadcast with Father Moran and the Swiss, when Emile pronounced the strip "a beauty." We expected no further trouble getting permission for a test landing (Figs. 27–29).

The most enjoyable part of each day was after dinner, when Ed usually held forth with stories of earlier expeditions, including many tales about the 1953 Everest Expedition that had never found their way into print and probably never will. There were also normally several rounds of songs, including interminable verses of Gilbert and Sullivan favorites, in which my New Zealand friends were unusually well versed.

Because Ed was (and still is) regarded as something of a beneficent local deity, we were feted almost everywhere we went, and the invariable serving of alcohol became oppressive after a while. When we arrived at Khumjung on the twenty-third, we were treated to an elaborate

Figs. 28 and 29. Lukla airstrip during one of the first test flights in 1964 (*top of page*) and in 1988, when the strip had been lengthened and the original hamlet had become a small town full of lodges, restaurants, shops, and government offices.

Fig. 30.   The Sherpas that Sir Edmund Hillary has assisted over the years treat him like a parent, almost a god.

reception at the school. All sorts of delicacies were served—curried eggs (chickens, now quite common, were then a rarity in Khumbu), potatoes, *nak*'s milk (*nak* is Sherpa for "female yak"), and of course the ubiquitous chang and *rakshi* (Figs. 30 and 31). It was a halcyon day— warm sun, no clouds, songs and dances by the school children. In the afternoon Ed and Max and I, in a light-headed stupor, got to work on the Khunde water tank while others headed for the mountain or the Namche school.

October 24:   Ed and I had a session in Khumjung with Tem Dorje, the Darjeeling Sherpa in charge of the so-called Hillary schools. Fortunately Ed was favorably inclined toward the suggestions I made in my report, so we are trying now to start a carpentry program and classes in traditional Tibetan painting. After more work on the water tank, I headed back to Namche by myself; dense mist was rolling in, and I headed blindly over the hill just for the fun of it since I know the area so well from commuting between Mingma's house in Khunde and Namche that there was no danger of getting lost. Brian Hearfield was hard at work on the Namche school floor, maintaining a higher standard of workmanship than I would have alone. The two of us had a good dinner, as we always do on this trip, and I have gained back plenty of weight. Mulgrew remarked the other day that four more men could have come along

Fig. 31.   Pemba Tharkay enjoys typically insistent Sherpa hospitality in 1964. By 1988 he had distinguished himself as a sardar on several expeditions, including assaults on the south face of Mt. Everest.

on what I have been eating, and Ed said I was the only person he had ever seen who could eat more *dal-bhat* than Jim Wilson. It's true that I usually stop eating only because I have to get on to other things.

October 26:   Emile came in and made a perfect landing, despite the ten-degree incline of our little strip. Actually this is an aid, since the slope slows the plane as it lands and helps it accelerate when it takes off—rather like going down a ski jump. The major difficulty is judging the height of the bottom of the strip as it comes up to meet you. Emile flew laterally across the bottom of the strip, set his altimeter, then circled around to come in straight for the actual landing. Of course a great deal of dirt and dust were blown into the air as he practiced takeoffs and landings. Packing down the surface had been the hardest part of building the Lukla strip—much more difficult than clearing the brush and leveling the terraces that were there. At one point we had tried dragging big heavy logs across it, but we finally found that the best method was to hire ten or fifteen Sherpas to walk (or run or dance, as they preferred) back and forth across it all day [Figs. 32 and 33]. By Sherpa standards this was easy work, and they enjoyed it immensely—singing and joking and laughing all the time they were at it. After a few days of this the earth was firm enough to take a plane landing.

The next day Ed and I went back up to the bridge site. Ed set a faster pace than I would normally have done, although it was not as fast as I was capable of going. I wondered what the hurry was and realized only

Figs. 32 and 33.   Groups of Sherpas help to pack down the airstrip.

later how competitive mountaineering can be—much more like competitive sports than I had thought. (By the 1980s attempts of extremely difficult and often near-suicidal routes undreamed of in the 1960s were necessary to establish one's reputation.) I wondered if he was racing me—no, that would be absurd; why should he bother? Rather he was

Fig. 34. The Namche school nears completion, with our tents beside it. The two translucent panels in the roof of the school let in ample diffused light even on an overcast day.

probably just testing himself, to see what he could handle at that stage of his life.

I sometimes took myself too seriously as the expedition expert on Nepal, Sherpas, village life, education, and local culture generally, forgetting that Ed had known about some of these things at a time when I had scarcely heard of the country. One night when Ed and I shared a tent at the bridge site, I must have put him to sleep with my explanation of the routes to Kathmandu before the Indian road was built—trails he had walked himself in those days. Although he sometimes seemed too hasty in deciding to do this or that in Khumbu, he usually turned out to be right. He had qualities that rumination and analytic deliberation on my part could not match: good instincts and shrewd judgment. (The world-famous figures I have met since that time have rarely lived up to expectations and have almost always disappointed in the flesh, but the more I got to know Ed, the more I admired him.)

Early in November Brian and I went up to Chhukung with the thought of climbing Island Peak, but we ran out of time and returned to the Namche school (Fig. 34) without attempting the mountain. We spent the next two weeks working on the Namche school; then on November 20 all of us (now including some members' wives, who had

Fig. 35. In his first attendance at an official function after his graduation from Eton, Prince (now King) Birendra hands out instructional materials to the new Chaurikharka students (the prince wears a white cloth cap).

arrived November 8) went to watch the Mani-Rimdu dances at Teng-boche. (It seems hard to imagine now, with thousands of tourists visiting Khumbu annually, that besides us there was only one other foreigner, a Danish trekker, there to see the ritual dancing in 1964.)

Later in November a large Russian helicopter landed in Khumjung; I helped the pilots to clear a straight path to give them the runway they would need to take off again at that altitude. As before at Dhankuta, despite our status as enemies, we recognized in each other cultural and technological affinities in the midst of Sherpa culture, which, however much I had grown to love and admire it, was clearly alien to us both.

We were all in Lukla on December 6 to welcome Crown Prince Bi-

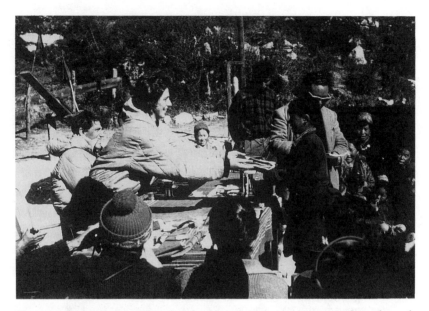

Fig. 36.   Lady Louise Hillary hands out prizes at a ceremony marking the end of the Khumjung school year in 1964. She and Belinda Hillary, one of the Hillarys' two daughters, were killed in a plane crash in Nepal in 1975. Their son, Peter, is an eminent mountaineer.

rendra when he arrived, in a great cloud of dust stirred up by the Russian helicopter, to inaugurate the Chaurikharka school (Fig. 35). He made a simple but effective speech to the villagers, emphasizing the brotherhood of all Nepalis. I walked back up to Lukla well in front of him so that I could photograph him hiking up the trail. It was all I could do to keep a respectable distance ahead of him; I was amazed at how fit and strong he was. I thought the altitude would have affected him, but he did not seem to notice the thin air and strode along as confidently as if he were at sea level.

December 9:   The expedition is winding down. I flew back to Kathmandu and helped wrap up matters by securing Mingma's passport from reluctant Singha Durbar officials. The maharajah of Sikkim and his American queen had invited the entire expedition to Gangtok at the conclusion of the expedition, but the Indian government would give permission only to the Hillarys, so the rest of us went our separate ways. The Unsoelds said Ed had told them that my work for the expedition was invaluable. I was glad to hear I had passed muster, since Ed is not inclined to hand out accolades very freely.

My job continued even after Ed and his wife, Louise, left, as I cleared various items back through customs again (Fig. 36). On the eighteenth

I flew to Delhi, then on to see my bride-to-be in Chicago (almost all the single members of the expedition married within the next few months), and finally home to Kentucky for Christmas.

I left Khumbu older and, I hope, wiser, but the longer I had stayed there, the more I had realized how little I understood of the Sherpa world. Although Sherpa culture seemed transparent and the people open, straightforward, and down-to-earth in a way easily grasped by a young American, I increasingly sensed vast differences between us in worldview, and many puzzles I had only begun to fathom. I hoped that anthropology, which I would begin studying the following fall, would help to unravel the mysteries. As I left, my only certainty about Khumbu was that I would ultimately return.

CHAPTER II

A Tradition of Change

Nepal packs more geographical and ecological diversity into fewer square miles than any other country in the world, and the people who inhabit this much-too-heavily populated land mirror that diversity. The country exhibits an unusually broad spectrum not only of geography but also of social, economic, religious, and linguistic types: from the flat-as-a-pancake rich farmland of the Tarai just above sea level along the Indian border in the south, with its full panoply of Hindu castes, its indigenous tribal groups, and its substantial Muslim minority, speaking Hindi, Urdu, Bhojpuri, and Maithili; through the terrace-laced middle hills, populated by farmers and herders ranging from Nepali-speaking high-caste Hindus—Brahmans and Chhetris—to such Mongoloid groups as Rais, Limbus, Gurungs, Magars, and Tamangs, all speaking Tibeto-Burman languages; to the high Himalayan valleys with their Buddhist, Tibetan-speaking nomads and settled farmers and traders. In the middle of all these is the Kathmandu Valley and its Newars—an ethnic universe unto itself. Nepal is, in anthropological jargon, a multiple society with plural cultures. The Sherpas who live in the high valleys in the southern shadow of Mt. Everest, in the Solu-Khumbu region of northeastern Nepal, are merely the most famous minority in a country where there is no majority.

Unlike most Nepalese, who are either Hindus by caste or tribes more or less Hinduized after centuries of prolonged contact and occasional intermarriage with Hindus, the Sherpas are unalloyed Buddhists. Indeed in religion, dress, language, kinship, marriage, and social life generally, they resemble the other people who live along either side of the five-hundred-mile northern border with Tibet. At the same time, however, the Sherpas are unique in all these dimensions, as they and outsiders readily agree.

The populations on the Nepal side of the frontier—which are culturally Tibetan but politically Nepalese—occupy about one-quarter of the total land area of Nepal, but they represent a numerically insignificant portion of the population. The Sherpas of Khumbu itself number fewer than 3,000; the total population of Nepal is more than 16 million. Another 17,000 Sherpas inhabit the area that fans south, east, and west of Khumbu, including the Sherpa strongholds of Solu and Pharak (the area below Namche Bazaar along the Dudh Koshi); they also live in Kathmandu and—a rather different strain of Sherpas—in the Helambu Valley just north of Kathmandu. Still other Sherpas—7,000 or so—live in Darjeeling, India, emigrants (or the descendants of emigrants) from Solu-Khumbu.[1]

The literal meaning of the word *Sherpa* is "easterner" (the Sherpa pronunciation is Sherwa, from *shar*, "east" and *wa*, "people"), and indeed some evidence indicates that Sherpas migrated to Solu-Khumbu some 450 years ago from the eastern Tibetan province of Kham, 1,250 miles away.[2] No one knows why they left Kham (perhaps to escape political upheavals or religious persecution), but it is not hard to imagine why they settled in Solu-Khumbu, where the topography, altitude, and climate were ideally suited to small-scale farming and the Sherpas' traditional pastoral nomadism.[3] Best of all, in those days it was empty, or at least nearly empty, and theirs for the taking.

Khumbu refers to the high-altitude area north of the confluence of the Bhote Koshi and Imja Khola; Solu, with its subregion Pharak, constitutes the southern, low-altitude portion of the region (see the map on p. xviii). Its six or so major villages and many smaller hamlets are perched high above the banks of these rivers or, in the case of Namche Bazaar, Khumjung, and Khunde, on the elevated land between them. Namche Bazaar is a little above 11,000 feet, and the other villages are all closer to 13,000 feet. Most of Khumbu consists of high-altitude rock, ice, and snow, and less than a fifth of 1 percent of it can be farmed (Figs. 37–40), but other land is suitable for pasture, water is plentiful, and wood is—or at least would have been 450 years ago—plentiful.

In Khumbu these Sherpa newcomers eventually established a routine of transhumance—farming the fields around their sturdy permanent houses and seasonally following their yak herds—to less substantial

Figs. 37 and 38. Agriculture has always formed the backbone of the Sherpa economy. As late as the 1950s teams of four men still occasionally pulled the ploughs that tilled the fields, but now animals do the work of pulling. The earlier photograph (*top of page*) is by Christoph von Fürer-Haimendorf.

Figs. 39 and 40.   Other aspects of agriculture remain the same, as Khumjung women use hoes to break up clods of dirt. The peak in the lower picture is Ama Dablam. The earlier photograph (*top of page*) is by Christoph von Fürer-Haimendorf.

shelters in higher pastures in summer and to lower ones in winter. In the high-altitude cold climate they could grow only bitter buckwheat, barley (but only in Dingboche, where there is adequate water), turnips, and coarse greens, relying on meat and dairy products (milk, yogurt, and cheese) from their cattle to supplement their vegetable diet. The yak and *nak* were crossed with lowland cattle and Tibetan cattle to produce the half-breed known as the *dzom* (which gives more milk than the *nak*) and its male counterpart, the *zopkio* (a more docile and tractable animal for plowing than the yak).

Many Sherpas made periodic trips via the almost-19,000-foot Nangpa La to barter grain for salt (and, to a lesser extent, wool). Namche Sherpas acquired a monopoly on this trade in 1828 (Ortner 1989) when the government in Kathmandu prohibited Solu and Pharak Sherpas from trading further north than Namche Bazaar and Tibetan traders from trading further south. Hence commerce was more important in Namche Bazaar than in any other Khumbu village, and agriculture and animal husbandry played minor roles there. This difference is instantly noticeable in the settlement pattern: Namche houses are closely clustered, with few fields around or among them; the houses in a village like Phortse, however, are separated from one another by large potato fields.

In the area of skilled labor and crafts Sherpas have operated largely at a low-technology, familial, do-it-yourself level. Weaving woolen cloth, building houses, repairing rope-sole boots—all these jobs the Sherpas either have done themselves or have hired others to do, depending on the level of their own skills, the size of the job, and competing demands on their time. Even the esoteric work of painting religious frescoes on the walls of monasteries or private chapels has not been a full-time profession. Before the development in the twentieth century of monasteries with full-time resident monks (see Ortner 1989), virtually everyone in Khumbu—including lamas, healers, and shamans in addition to skilled craftsmen—must have either worked the land, or herded yak, or engaged in trade, or worked for those who practiced these traditional occupations.

The small initial population (by 1836 there were still only 169 households in Khumbu, compared with 596 in 1957; see Fürer-Haimendorf 1964) probably grew at a barely perceptible rate for the first three hundred or so years. This demographic calm was upset by the introduction of the potato (not to be confused with an indigenous tuber called *tho* by the Sherpas, which was used to make noodles) around the middle of the nineteenth century. The potato's high productivity signaled a quantum leap in crop yields on the .19 percent of Khumbu land that is arable. It is now the dominant crop, accounting for 90 percent of all planted fields, with buckwheat (5 percent), vegetables (4 percent), and barley (1 percent) making up the balance.

The new food source appears to have attracted a second wave of Tibetan immigration and an accelerated flow of poor Tibetan migrants in the following decades. By the turn of the century Khumbu had begun to fill up. Even before then, beginning about the 1850s, Sherpas had begun traveling to Darjeeling to seek their fortunes after the British began building roads and tea plantations there. Thus Sherpas were both "pushed" and "pulled" to emigrate. When a doctor from Glasgow named Kellas began climbing in the Sikkimese Himalaya in 1907, he was able to draw on a pool of Sherpa porters in Darjeeling who had moved there from Solu-Khumbu (Mason [1955] gives the history of Himalayan mountaineering). By 1922 there were some fifty Sherpas employed by the British in their first attempt on Mt. Everest.[4] The most famous of these Khumbu immigrants to Darjeeling (though he was born in Tibet) was Tenzing Norgay, who with Edmund Hillary made the first ascent of Mt. Everest in 1953.

Not only agriculture and animal husbandry but also religious observances such as Mani-Rimdu; communal rituals such as *Osho,* which protects village fields from malignant forces; and community celebrations such as the village feast *Dumje,* with different residents serving as hosts in turn, follow a pattern set largely by the passage of the seasons. In recent years such changes as employment in mountaineering and trekking have adapted themselves to this annual cycle, as shown in Figure 41.

In most respects life after the introduction of the potato and the availability of new employment opportunities in Darjeeling must have gone on much as before, but these economic shifts allowed Khumbu to support a larger population, some of whom could be spared the burden of pursuing traditional means of livelihood. Strong village political organization (see pp. 62–63) combined with an equally strong Buddhist ideology allowed the Sherpas to collect and concentrate their wealth in religious activities in a more substantial and visible way than previously. The Sherpas had been Buddhists at least since the middle of the seventeenth century and supported temples (*gompas*) attended by local married lamas in most villages. Only in the twentieth century did they begin to build and staff substantial monasteries like those in Tengboche

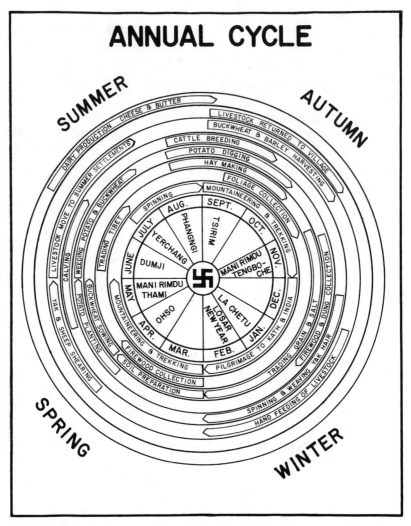

Fig. 41. The Sherpa annual cycle. Adapted from Mingma Norbu Sherpa 1985.

and Thame (which belong to the unreformed, "red-hat," Nyingmapa sect),[5] with full-time, celibate monks. (Tengboche was constructed in 1916 and rebuilt after the 1933 earthquake.) Subsequently many Sherpa men spent a few years learning to read Tibetan in a monastery, even if they eventually left it to marry and lead secular lives. As a result, Sherpa literacy rates—estimated at one-third of the adult male population (Fürer-Haimendorf 1960)—have been uncharacteristically high for such a remote Nepalese area.

Prior to this twentieth-century religious surge, the practice of Buddhism was limited to services conducted in the village temple by village lamas and the life-cycle rituals conducted at home—those associated with such events as birth, marriage, and death. According to Ortner, all such local religious services "have a broadly common structure, centering on offerings and petitions to the gods, and offerings and threats to the demons, and closing with a distribution of ritual foods to all present" (1978, 32). These rituals reflect the significance of hospitality and reciprocity generally in Sherpa social relations. Another dimension of village religion is the communication with spirits by shamans (called *lhawa* by the Sherpas) under trance. The shaman's goal is more to determine the cause of illness than to cure it. One of several possible treatments is to feed whatever spirit has caused the illness, thereby equalizing or at least stabilizing relations between the human and supernatural worlds.

To be a "true" Sherpa nowadays is to belong to one of about eighteen (depending on how you count them) patrilineal, exogamous clans. (The original migrants, according to Oppitz [1968, 144], belonged to only four "protoclans," which have since divided into additional units.) The Sherpa population in the Khumbu villages has been augmented by a trickle of clanless Tibetans (locally called Khamba, although they do not pretend to come from Kham) who have crossed over into Khumbu over the centuries. Those who have settled into Khumbu villages, acquired wealth, and become generally absorbed into Sherpa society (often intermarrying with someone from a Sherpa clan) are also loosely referred to as Sherpas, as are those who are descendants of alliances between Sherpas or Khambas and other ethnic groups, such as Newars, Tamangs, or Chhetris. In addition to restricting the range of potential marriage partners, these clans have only a few small and relatively unimportant ritual functions, including occasional group worship of clan deities. They are not now political or economic corporate groups, though Ortner (1978, 19) speculates that in Solu, at least, they might originally have been.

Since Khumbu villages are multiclan units, individuals can often find a suitable marriage partner from within their own village. Marriage itself is not an event as we normally think of it in the West but rather an economic process, with little religious significance, that takes several years to consummate. Some marriages are arranged by the parents, but even these arranged marriages are often merely de facto approvals of unions initiated by the open courtship of the principals. Indeed, a girl may even be courted in her own house by a boy who climbs through the window in the dark of night and leaves before the parents discover him in the morning.

A formal engagement is called *sodhne* ("to ask" in Nepali), but even at this stage exclusive sexual rights cannot be demanded, and such engagements are frequently broken off before the commencement of the next stage, *dem-chang* ("beer of mixing" in Sherpa). *Dem-chang* signals a more serious legal commitment: any children born after *dem-chang* are legitimate, and the dissolution of the relationship after this point requires the same payments that must be made in divorce after the final wedding rites, known as *zendi* (the spelling reflects the Sherpa pronunciation of the Nepali term *janti*). Parents help Sherpa couples to establish their own separate households if they can, the parental house going to the youngest son by the rule of ultimogeniture.

Young children are indulged their every whim and, as elsewhere in Nepal, older ones take care of younger ones. As soon as they are able, children begin helping with the chores of the house, boys looking after cattle and girls helping their mothers around the house and in the fields, though girls help with cattle too if they have no brothers. As they contribute more and more to the running of the household, they are treated increasingly as adults. Unlike children in the West, Sherpa children are always participants in parties and festivities. Thus no aspect of adult life is strange to them by the time they are grown. Sherpa children are not "raised" so much as merely lived with.

Tied together by clan, kin, and marriage, Khumbu Sherpas as of the 1950s were also part of a community bound together by civic institutions designed to deal with many of the collective wants and needs of the village. In each village a small number of men (two in Khumjung) called *nawas* were responsible for controlling the use of village land for agriculture and cattle. This task involved enforcing village-wide bans on cattle, sheep, and goats from cultivated land until the crops had been harvested. New *nawas* were elected each year, ostensibly by a village assembly but in reality by a few village leaders in informal consultation. In addition to the *nawas* who controlled the movement of cattle and coordinated work in the fields, there was another type of *nawa*, called *shing* (wood) *nawa*, in charge of protecting forests near the village. Each village elected three or four *shing nawas* to protect its forests from unauthorized woodcutters. These *nawas* could give permission to fell trees for special purposes such as house building, but they guarded against unnecessary deforestation. Finally, the *chorumba* and *chorpen* were responsible for the upkeep of the *gompa,* the performance of religious rites, the organization and discipline of village festivals such as *Dumje,* and the administration of village funds earmarked for *gompa* purposes. Basically these civic roles were filled by rotation among established village families, but other, less important, positions were rotated among all villagers. The rotation of leadership is important in that it provides the potential for frequent innovation.

Regardless of the importance of the particular office, the guiding principle for the governing of a Sherpa village was essentially democratic:

Authority is vested in the totality of its inhabitants. This authority is then delegated to officials elected for limited periods, and during the term of their office they may be guided by decisions on policy made by a public gathering but are not responsible to any superior body for the day to day administration of agreed rules. They have power to inflict fines and collect them as well as to grant exemption from general rules in case of individual hardship. The village community as a whole cannot correct the actions of such an official, but can only express disapproval by withholding re-election or any future appointment. (Fürer-Haimendorf 1964, 104)

Two other events of the 1950s further affected life in Khumbu. When mountaineering expeditions inside Nepal began, Khumbu Sherpas seeking work as high-altitude porters no longer had to go to Darjeeling, for most of the expeditions were organized in Kathmandu, and porters and Sherpas were hired there. Employment with these expeditions, which attempted peaks all over Nepal, reduced the economic pressure to go to Darjeeling and presumably helped stanch the flow of migrants from Khumbu to India. It also eventually forced the recognition that Khumbu Sherpas were divided from their Darjeeling cousins by citizenship: the former were Nepalese, the latter Indian. No one had ever thought this an issue, let alone a problem, until 1953, when both India and Nepal bitterly tried to claim Tenzing Norgay as their own.

The second event of the 1950s that altered life in Khumbu was the incursion and the vastly expanded power of the Chinese in Tibet. Two consequences followed from the increased Chinese control. First, the flow of trade over the Nangpa La was drastically curtailed. Some of the small-scale bartering of grain for salt was allowed to continue in central depots under Chinese control. With trade by weight instead of volume, however, and with bargaining outlawed, there was less profit. The Chinese authorities also largely brought a halt to big-time trading in hides, sugar, wool, jewelry, butter, and cattle. This curtailment threatened to severely dislocate the Namche Bazaar economy, where fortunes had been routinely made on the Nangpa La monopoly.

The second result of the Chinese occupation of Tibet was the enormous influx of refugees into Khumbu following the flight of the Dalai Lama from Lhasa in 1959 (Fig. 42). At one point in the early 1960s over 6,000 Tibetan refugees—far more than the total number of tourists in a single year in the 1980s—lived in Khumbu, along with the normal Sherpa population of that time of just over 2,200. Many of the yak and sheep died, and most of the refugees moved on to other locations in Nepal and India or eventually returned to Tibet. Only about ten refugee families settled in Khumbu, where they have gradually become integrated into established Sherpa society.

Although they were absorbed into Sherpa society, these Tibetans also affected Khumbu life. For example, the traditional Sherpa stove consisted of an open fire with three stones (later an iron tripod) supporting the cooking vessel. The Tibetan refugees of 1959 and after brought with them the technological innovation of an enclosed multiburner hearth of stone and mud. The traditional Sherpa stove, only 6–8 percent efficient, has been largely replaced in Khumbu houses by the enclosed stove, which is 30–80 percent efficient (Mingma Norbu Sherpa 1985, 180).

Sherpa history thus has not been static. Ever since the forebears' departure from eastern Tibet at the end of the fifteenth century, Sherpa society has been changing—with the arrival and settlement in Khumbu, the increase in number of clans, the adoption of Buddhism, the building of village temples, the introduction of the potato, the large growth in population, the emigration to Darjeeling, the establishment of celibate monasteries, and employment in mountaineering. The customary commonsense distinction between "tradition" and "change" is therefore ultimately untenable. Rather there is, and always has been in Sherpa society, a "tradition of change."

There is a distinction, however, between the cumulative, compounding change I have described and the changes that began in the 1960s. Before then changes were primarily those of scale and elaboration: more clans, more food, more people, more trade (until it was curtailed in 1959), more lamas, more rituals (and more elaborate rituals), more differentiation (as traders and tax collectors accumulated wealth), more emigration. These changes, however fundamental, were also of a piece with the Tibetan cultural cloth from which Sherpa culture had been cut. The intensified religious activity in the twentieth century, for example,

Fig. 42. The polyandry practiced by these Tibetans, one of the few refugee families that settled in Khumbu, differs from the fraternal polyandry of the Sherpas. The polyandrous marriage of two brothers (1 and 3) to the woman (2) produced a child (5) who acknowledges both men equally as his fathers. Subsequently 1 took 4 as a second wife, and later 5 also married 4. The kinship diagram describes these relationships. The numbers, beginning at left with 1, correspond to the individuals in the photograph.

in a way simply enabled the Sherpas to "catch up" with the level of religiosity achieved long before in the Tibetan homeland: the monasteries at Tengboche and Thame, for example, were established as branches of Rongbuk Monastery on the other side of Mt. Everest.

It is true that by the end of the eighteenth century Khumbu had also come under the control of the state of Nepal, which appointed some Sherpas as *pembu*, "tax collectors," to represent state interests. But day-to-day life must have been little changed. For example, when a group of "judges" was sent to Solu-Khumbu in 1805 to enforce the Hindu ban on cow slaughter (yak and yak crossbreeds counted as cattle for this purpose), the Sherpas readily confessed their crime and were fined. The Hindu judges reported back to the government that if the penalty of death or enslavement were imposed, many people would be executed or enslaved (Stiller 1973; Regmi 1979; Ortner 1989). The Sherpa diet remained unaffected.

The changes since 1961 have been different. The construction and operation of elementary schools in all Khumbu villages by the end of the 1960s brought literacy not in Tibetan but in Nepali and English; the establishment of a hospital in Khunde in 1966 had such wide-ranging effects as the virtual elimination of such thyroid deficiency diseases as cretinism and goiter (the latter had had an incidence of 92 percent) and a reduction in population growth through contraceptive measures; an airstrip constructed in 1964 at Lukla shortened the travel time from Kathmandu to Khumbu from two weeks to forty minutes, and eventually funneled into Khumbu more than six thousand tourists per year; and establishment of the panchayat system in the 1960s and of Sagarmatha National Park in 1975 effectively ended several centuries of regional political autonomy.

Although these post-1961 changes have in some ways fundamentally realigned the ecological, economic, and political pillars of Sherpa society, in other respects they have had little effect on "traditional" Sherpa institutions, some of which have continued much as before. In some cases the changes have actually intensified Sherpa life and made it "more Sherpa" than ever. The remaining chapters attempt to sort out, describe, interrelate, and explain these changes and their myriad effects on Sherpa life.

CHAPTER III

Schools for Sherpas

In all countries of the Third World central planners agree on the need for bigger and better educational efforts. A good educational system can shore up the fragile self-confidence of embattled elites. In addition, however, education is supposed to inculcate those skills that will help the population to develop "an industrial, processing and diversified agricultural economy," as well as to "produce a modern nation of dedicated citizens from a population of peasants who have small experience and understanding of civic, consensual or mobilization politics" (Nash 1965, 131). Statistical surveys document the achievement of these objectives (though the statistics are often more fanciful than factual), detailing the number of school-age children in school, the availability of instructional materials, and, most important, the rate of literacy. The ways in which village schools function "on the ground," that is, in their social and cultural settings, are not so well understood.

Unlike universities, village schools are "numerous, decentralized, less open for inspection, less amenable to manipulation, and most importantly, they are set into local communities" (Nash 1965, 131). But it is also true that when compared with other, less tangible, aspects of Third World rural life, village schools are institutions that are conspicuously organized, related to the national matrix in definite bureaucratic ways, and subject to central planning efforts.

What makes the Sherpa case so intriguing is the existence of traditional "schools"—that is, Buddhist monasteries—long before anything like the present system of village schools was dreamed of. In monasteries like Tengboche the *thawas* (novice monks) receive religious instruction and study sacred Buddhist texts, all of which are written in classical Tibetan, a language that bears about the same affinity to modern spoken Tibetan as Latin does to Italian. The population of the monasteries is not static, and Fürer-Haimendorf estimated in the 1950s that about 50 percent of all entering monks eventually marry and return to village life. This explains why until very recently roughly a third of adult Sherpa males have been literate in Tibetan.

It is quite usual for laymen to join the lamas in the readings from books during temple or domestic ceremonies, and many households possess at least a few books. Most moral, spiritual, and intellectual inspiration comes ultimately from the monastery, which thus shares with the pilgrim center in India the capacity to "influence the way of life of everyone in its hinterland" (Srinivas 1966, 23). In short, the monastery touches on almost all aspects of Sherpa life, and the image of the educated person as highly esteemed is well established. The monastery is, to apply to it the characterization Geertz applied to Islamic schools in Indonesia, "the master institution in the perpetuation of the [Buddhist] tradition and the creation of a [Buddhist] society" (1963, 10). Unlike the Indonesian Islamic schools, however, the monasteries were never traditionally concerned with efforts to modernize Sherpa society.

THE HILLARY SCHOOLS

In this traditional cultural and educational setting Sir Edmund Hillary in 1960 asked some Sherpas how he could repay them for the indispensable role they had played in the several mountaineering expeditions he had participated in and led. They answered that they wanted schools for their children, who, as the Thame Sherpas later put it, "have eyes but still they are blind" (Hillary 1964, 3).

One of the objectives of that year's expedition was to solve the mystery of the yeti. Sir Edmund proposed to take the yeti scalp kept in the Khumjung *gompa* around the world for examination by scientists in leading museums and universities, in return for which he would compensate the Sherpas. Various proposals for compensation were discussed, including a cash fee and the donation of a new roof for the *gompa*. Some high-altitude Sherpas on the expedition argued that they needed education more than anything else, and the view that the construction of a village school would be the most timely quid pro quo eventually prevailed.

Fig. 43.   I lived for several months in 1974 in this room (a dilapidated chapel) at one end of Wangchu Lama's house in Khumjung. Since then the house and the chapel have been renovated.

Wangchu Lama, a Solu native who had married into Khumjung and become a leading citizen there (Fig. 43), wrote a petition (he was probably the only Sherpa in all of Khumbu who was literate in Nepali at the time) asking for a school for the forty to fifty school-age children living in the village. He affixed to it the thumbprints of their parents and told his son Kalden to carry the petition to the village of Milingo to await Sir Edmund's arrival from the airstrip at Mingbo. Sir Edmund agreed to the terms of the petition and also asked Wangchu for permission to take Kalden to Kathmandu to enroll him in the Jesuit boarding school there so that he could eventually return as a teacher. Wangchu agreed, and so Kalden, with the scalp, set out for Kathmandu on foot with the small Hillary party—a trip that would transform his own life as well as the lives of future generations of Khumbu children (Figs. 44 and 45).

Thus was born what would become the Sherpa village school system. Providing material assistance to the people of the area was not unprecedented, however. The British Everest Expedition of 1922 had delivered a load of cement to the abbot of Rongbuk Monastery on the north side of Everest to repair the buildings there.

Wangchu's interest in education is explained partly by his Solu ori-

Figs. 44 and 45. Kalden, the first Khumbu Sherpa to be educated, returned to Khumjung in 1963 after two years in Father Moran's boarding school in Kathmandu. By 1964 (*top of page*) he had married and had a son, Sonam. By 1988 he owned a prosperous trekking agency in Kathmandu; he had contributed generously to the financial support of the Sherpa religion; and he had fathered five more children by a second wife. He stands (*above*) before his nearly completed palatial modern hotel in Lukla, built at a cost of some $200,000, all from his own resources.

gins; a native Khumbu Sherpa might not have immediately thought of or supported so wholeheartedly the idea of a village school, at least not initially. Twenty-five years later Wangchu and others still have to persuade some parents to let their children continue in school—either locally or at a college elsewhere in Nepal. Even students who have done well and gone on to higher education on scholarships are sometimes confronted by skeptical parents who urge them to give up school and do something useful and, above all, profitable. This attitude is attuned to the local wisdom that advocates working with tourists—with the ultimate aim of being a powerful, influential, and well-paid sardar—rather than going to school (and perhaps becoming overeducated). The high fatality rate on mountaineering expeditions, which offer another means of earning money, also works to funnel Sherpas toward the tourist industry.

The fact that lamas spend many years studying—the more years the better—does not affect the Sherpas' ideas about the length of time their children should spend in secular schools. Religious learning is cumulative (it carries over even from previous lives), and because it concerns the central point of life—salvation—it is impossible to overdo. Secular education, by contrast, is considered useful to the extent that it teaches basic literacy and arithmetic, both valuable skills for competing in the larger society. But most Khumbu Sherpas see little point in continuing on into the higher grades, let alone college.

Sir Edmund's response to a series of requests for help from different villages has been to raise funds (originally from Field Enterprises and its subsidiary World Book Encyclopedia; from Sears; and, increasingly, from the governments of Canada and New Zealand and organizations such as the British Venture Scouts, who raised £175,000 in the fall of 1988) through what is now called the Himalayan Trust to build, supply, maintain, and, originally, staff schools in some sixteen villages in Solu, Khumbu, and other nearby areas. He has given piecemeal assistance—a new room here, a new roof there—to half a dozen other schools.[1]

The first school, built in 1961 in Khumjung, expanded over the years to include all grades from first through tenth, the last year of high school in the Nepalese secondary school system (Figs. 46–48). In 1963 two more elementary schools were built, one in Pangboche and the other in Thame (Fig. 49). In the autumn of 1964 the Himalayan Schoolhouse Expedition (see chapter 1) built three more schools: one in the Solu Village of Junbesi; one in Chaurikharka, just below the Lukla airstrip; and one in Namche Bazaar.

Fig. 46. The one-room Khumjung school (*below center, right*) was built of aluminum sections.

Fig. 47. The expanded Khumjung campus in 1988 included classrooms for all ten grades as well as a separate library and a principal's office.

Fig. 48. The principal of Khumjung school, Shyam Pradhan, teaches a class in the original schoolhouse. The boy in the second row, left, is Ang Thukten, whom his parents (Konjo Chumbi and his wife) called Philip because he was born on the trail while they were walking from Khumjung to Kathmandu to meet Queen Elizabeth and Prince Philip on their royal visit to Nepal in 1961. Konjo had visited Buckingham Palace in 1960 when he accompanied Sir Edmund Hillary on his trip around the world with a yeti scalp (see p. 68 and Plate 10).

In their curriculum, schedule, pedagogy, and day-to-day operation, what have become popularly known as the Hillary schools are much like other elementary schools in Nepal, but they also possess some unique advantages. Although they are hopelessly distant from any source of electricity (not counting the recently established small hydro-electric system in Namche Bazaar), the sturdy corrugated-aluminum roofs contain translucent plastic panels that admit a diffused light ample for reading and writing on even the dreariest day. The teachers were originally better qualified and better paid than teachers in village schools elsewhere in Nepal; now, however, they are paid according to the government's standard teacher's scale. But the Hillary schools continue to be better provided with equipment, books, and other teaching materials.

The language of instruction is the national language, Nepali, an Indo-Aryan lingua franca that roughly half of all Nepalese speak as

Fig. 49.   A used oxygen bottle from a Mt. Everest expedition is struck to signal the beginning of the school day at the Thame school.

their mother tongue. The Sherpas' own language belongs to the entirely unrelated Sino-Tibetan family of languages. It is closely related to Tibetan, but Tibetan speakers cannot understand it. Traditionally, most adult male Sherpas, from their trading expeditions and travel, understood and spoke (but could not read or write) passable Nepali. Outside of the schools, however, Nepali is heard spoken only with tourists' porters, government personnel, and so on.

In addition to Nepali, the curriculum of the schools (see appendix B) includes such subjects as arithmetic, elementary science and hygiene, geography, history, and English—the normal fare at any Nepalese ele-

mentary school. Maps of the country are conspicuous, and the ubiquitous portraits of their majesties the king and queen of Nepal adorn the
walls of each school. Thus in several different ways these new schools
represent organizational and symbolic extensions of a hitherto alien
national society.

In the beginning the staffs of the schools mediated and mitigated the
foreignness of these new institutions. The teachers were mostly Sherpas
who had been born, reared, and educated in Darjeeling, India, the cosmopolitan hill station just ten miles from the Nepalese border. Most
were descendants of migrants from Solu-Khumbu two or three generations back. They were seen by the Khumbu population as Sherpas who
had gone into the wider world and succeeded in it.

Although they were Sherpas, they spoke Sherpa only about as well
as the average American Jew speaks Hebrew: not very well. Their first
language was Nepali, and they had received at least a high school education in Nepali-speaking schools. Legally Indian nationals, they nonetheless felt, as Nepali speakers from a Nepal-India border town, a kinship with Nepal not shared by other Indians. Since they also looked to
Solu-Khumbu as their fatherland, they were eager and proud to serve
as bicultural brokers between the two traditions to which they belonged. These Nepalized Sherpas maintained an empathetic attitude toward their distant mountain cousins and were therefore able to mediate
sympathetically between the villagers and the foreign culture of education. The teacher at Thame in 1964, for example, carefully explained
the value of the schools to skeptical parents in terms they could understand. He argued that literacy in Nepali would enable them to read
letters from outside Khumbu, whether of a friendly or a commercial
nature, and help them avoid being cheated by tax collectors, unscru-
pulous merchants, and the like. As an educated man he was listened to,
but because he was a Sherpa, his innovative behavior was less at odds
with local ways than that of a teacher from a different cultural tradition
would have been.

Now that the schools have taken root, only two Darjeeling Sherpa
teachers are left in Khumbu. All the others are non-Sherpa Nepalese
from elsewhere in Nepal. The allure of trekking jobs has made it impossible to recruit local educated Sherpas as teachers in Khumbu (this
issue is pursued further in chapter 4).

In general, the Hillary schools have much more in common with
secondary schools elsewhere in Nepal than with the monasteries of
Khumbu. Common to all these village schools is an emphasis on rote

learning and a conception of education that regards all knowledge, whether validated by the authority of the teacher or the text, as known and waiting to be memorized.

The curricula of the schools and monasteries have nothing in common, the monasteries relying exclusively on the traditional subjects of Buddhist texts. Whereas school texts are mastered to pass exams, Buddhist texts are mastered because they are inherently powerful. Other traditional Sherpa learning processes (such as those involving healing and tantric powers) also rely on the transmission of power. The monks tend to know less Nepali (and less about Nepal) than the average villager, whether or not he or she has ever been to school. In short, village schools, utilizing a language completely different from the local tongue, located in villages (unlike monasteries), and representing a national political system and ideology, are a novel institution in Khumbu.

Given all these differences, what prompted the Sherpas to request schools in the first place? Left entirely to their own devices, villages like Khumjung would have had no school at all. Even now they are no more self-sufficient than any other Nepalese village school. In each case the Sherpas donated the land for their school and all the unskilled labor required to build it, but they contribute virtually nothing to the ongoing operational expenses, which are handled entirely by Sir Edmund Hillary's Himalayan Trust and His Majesty's Government. The Sherpas realized early on that although they had never needed special institutions to learn how to become Sherpas—the traditional avenues of socialization and enculturation were enough for that—they needed modern schools if they were to have hopes of dealing with the outside world in any but a subordinate, submissive way.

The motivation behind the requests for schools was therefore straightforward: the economic reasons mentioned by the Thame teacher (which became more cogent as commercial ventures became increasingly oriented to Nepal rather than Tibet) along with a dash of desire for the prestige associated with education in Nepal and the increasingly clear understanding that future political lines of force were going to be drawn toward the rest of Nepal, not Tibet.

In Khumbu the combination of village secular schools and monastic "schools" now permits most people who want an education to acquire at least some exposure to it. One clear measure of the schools' importance is the number of children attending. In 1964 roughly half the eligible Khumjung children attended school. In 1974 about two-thirds of those eligible attended; 67 of 111 Khumjung houses had school-age children; 43 of the 67 houses sent a total of 73 children to school, and 36 children, distributed among 24 houses, did not attend. Some of these children had attended school in the past; their parents felt that they had received a basic education and acquired the knowledge they needed for the work they were likely to do and the life they were likely to live.

Parental attitudes are ambivalent. Those who did not send their children to school expressed concern about their children's not being educated; that is, they perceived education as an important component of raising their children. But they also felt that enough is enough. For example, although Ang Rita stood first in all Nepal on the School Leaving Certificate (S.L.C.) exam required for high school graduation and won several scholarships to study elsewhere in Nepal and to attend college outside the country, his mother could see little point in education beyond the simple three R's and tried, unsuccessfully, to persuade her son to give up further schooling. Attrition in the early 1970s increased markedly in the upper grades, leaving only five students in what was then the top grade, the seventh.

The society has so far not been fragmented by differential access to new knowledge and institutions, except to the extent that poverty dictates enrollment percentages. The primary reasons parents did not send their children to school were economic or domestic. That is, the child either had to work to keep the family economy going—by looking after animals, for example (Fig. 50)—or was needed to look after the younger children at home. Even with all materials, including pencils and paper, provided free (a level of support not available in other Nepalese secondary schools), many children cannot be spared from various domestic or economic tasks. (In some cases—the numerous children who are cretins, for example—the children simply have no interest in attending or their parents have no such interest on their behalf.) Ultimately the Hillary program was obliged to pay stipends of Rs 100–150 per month to students attending grades six through ten of the Khumjung school; these stipends account to a considerable extent for the higher enrollment percentages now achieved. These stipends, the virtual guarantee of a college scholarship for anyone who passes the S.L.C. exam in the second division or above, and the generally high quality of the Khumjung high school now attract not only Khumbu Sherpas but also high-caste Hindus from villages several days' walk to the south.

Those who do not drop out do very well in the national high school examinations. In 1984 the first batch of students to complete tenth

Fig. 50. Not all children can be spared from domestic chores. This boy, shepherd for a flock of sheep in a nearby pasture, looks enviously through the school's window at his friends in class.

grade in Khumjung graduated. Of the ten students, one girl decided to postpone taking the S.L.C. exam until the following year because her father had died recently, and one boy failed. The remaining eight students were boys—five Sherpas and three "down valley Nepalese"—who took and passed the exam, most of them in the first division. All eight enrolled in colleges in Kathmandu, supported by Himalayan Trust Scholarships. Few, if any, other Nepalese high schools, including the best private schools, could boast this kind of success.

That nine out of ten graduates in 1984 were boys is characteristic of the imbalance of the sexes in the upper classes. Enrollments in 1986

TABLE 1   KHUMJUNG SCHOOL ENROLLMENTS, 1986

Grade level	Boys	(%)	Girls	(%)	Total
	Primary				
First	46	(46)	55	(54)	101
Second	21	(60)	14	(40)	35
Third	19	(59)	13	(41)	32
Fourth	12	(48)	13	(52)	25
Fifth	18	(82)	4	(18)	22
TOTAL	116	(54)	99	(46)	215
	Lower secondary				
Sixth	15	(58)	11	(42)	26
Seventh	19	(83)	4	(17)	23
TOTAL	34	(69)	15	(31)	49
	Secondary				
Eighth	27	(79)	7	(21)	34
Ninth	26	(100)	0	(0)	26
Tenth	19	(95)	1	(5)	20
TOTAL	72	(90)	8	(10)	80
TOTALS	222	(65)	122	(35)	344

(Table 1) show the same pattern. In the elementary grades the number of boys and girls is about equal. In the upper grades the number of girl students (and thus female graduates) diminishes sharply. Sherpa girls, like other Nepalese women, receive less education than boys. The reason is not that daughters must help at home with jobs that sons cannot do—many jobs (carrying firewood, working in the fields) sons could do at least as well as daughters, if not better. Rather, parents think that a high school diploma is unnecessary for their daughters, who are likely to be wives and mothers, whereas higher education for their sons can yield big payoffs in tourism. The male orientation of Sherpa society is also seen in the great joy expressed at the birth of a boy and the distinct lack of enthusiasm shown at the birth of a girl.

As culturally, linguistically, and politically extrinsic institutions, the schools are inherently agents of change. Returning to Khumjung after its school had been in operation for less than two years, Sir Edmund Hillary observed change that was "superficial," perhaps, but constituted

change nonetheless. Instead of faces and hands coated with years of dirt and soot, they were clean and glowed with the flush of perfect health; instead of dirty, torn clothing, their garments showed at least some attempt at tidiness and care. . . . After school hours you could walk through the village and see ample signs of the children's enthusiasm for their new education. Out of an open window would come drifting, childish voices practicing reading or learning arithmetic tables. Or you'd pass a couple of students sitting cross-legged in the field in front of their home, writing line after line of flowing Nepali with the dedication of any scholar. (Hillary 1964, 22–23)

The schools and their personnel are detached from prevailing norms and social arrangements, but whether they have fomented fundamental cultural change is a different, more serious, question.

Whether the schools become agents of large-scale cultural change depends on how they mesh with the other institutions and values of Sherpa life. Both the schools and the monasteries fulfill educational functions, but their curricula are entirely different. Rather than students learning, say, both a scientific and a Buddhist cosmology and believing only the Buddhist (as happens in Burmese schools), one set of students (village children) learns the content of one curriculum and another set (novice monks) learns another. In the confrontation (or, more accurately, the mutual ignoring) of two entirely different educational traditions, could a political, linguistic, or knowledge gap develop between the monks and lay villagers? If some kind of social Gresham's law operates in these circumstances, might the monastery become the institution of less repute and hence slowly fade from the scene?

In 1964 I formulated two mutually contradictory answers to this question. First, the modernizing efforts of the schools would be ineffectual against the strong tide of monastic influence. Second, because oral traditions are relatively underdeveloped, Sherpa society as it was then constituted could be shattered by the decay of monastic education and the resulting decline in the transmission of culture. Such drastic change has already been reported among the Thakali along the Kali-Gandaki River north of Pokhara. There, Thakali children who had been sent to schools in large Hindu towns (and many Sherpa children have graduated from high schools in such towns) subsequently returned to their homes and attempted to desecrate and destroy Buddhist gompas (Bista 1971).[2]

Even without such unsettling repercussions, Khumbu lamas would to some extent be excluded from the integrative processes taking place in and through the schools that were linking the region with the rest of the kingdom. Thus the lamas themselves would gradually be isolated from the rest of Nepal and their own Sherpa villages (their traditionally strong ties in Tibet, where institutional Buddhism was being effectively destroyed, had already been cut).

Because of this gulf that seemed likely to develop on one or more fronts, I recommended in my 1964 report to Sir Edmund that the schools and the monasteries be more integrated than they were. I encouraged the Tengboche rimpoche both to organize a school at the monastery that would teach Western subjects and to make Tengboche a center of Buddhist activity by printing woodblock editions of sacred texts and supporting other traditional Buddhist scholarly activity. Ideally the school, attended by the novitiates, would combine the political enculturation of schools in the villages with the traditional monastic regime of Tengboche. To this end, beginning in 1965, Sir Edmund has assisted the rimpoche from time to time in his educational efforts; a new school was finally built in 1987. The progressive ideas of the rimpoche were stymied for a while by conservative elements within the *gompa,* and later the district school inspector ruled that Tibetan could not be taught during regular school hours. Moreover, the Tengboche and Thame rimpoches feel, probably correctly, that teaching English to the monks will encourage some of the less devout to leave the *gompa* and perhaps pursue careers in trekking. The net result has been that the Tengboche school lacks the "integrationist" slant I had envisaged for it.

Parts of the idea are now being put into practice at the Sherpa Cultural Center at Tengboche. The center houses a library with books in several languages on the religion, history, and culture of Khumbu as well as a museum display of Sherpa crafts and both secular and religious artifacts. A sign reads, School—Library—Museum—Appropriate Development. As the rimpoche admits, at present the museum is basically for foreigners, but in the future it will increasingly instruct Sherpas about their past. Authentic bicultural training of monks (*thawas*), however, has yet to be realized institutionally.

When I recommended the partial secularization of the monastery, I also suggested that the village schools teach traditional Sherpa activities as a step toward integrating the schools with traditional Sherpa culture (Fig. 51). Although, as I have already mentioned, Sherpas traditionally can learn to be Sherpas by growing up in their own social system, some skills, such as Tibetan religious painting and carpentry, are not widely known. After the decline of Buddhism in Tibet, religious painting in particular was in danger of becoming esoteric. Carpentry was to be taught (a separate carpentry shop was subsequently built for this purpose) in part so that what Geertz called the moral significance of honest sweat would not be lost in an inundation of academic subjects. I hoped that the chance to learn such subjects as carpentry, weaving, and Tibetan painting might entice into the schools children wanting to know

Fig. 51. Traditional Sherpa weaving is taught at the school.

more about the art of being a Sherpa. By 1986 the carpentry building had been transformed into the school library, but weaving was still being taught.

COGNITIVE DEVELOPMENT

One approach to measuring the impact of the schools is to determine what the students are learning. An obvious way to do that would be simply to list what they have studied (see appendix B) and assume that is what they know—as long as they pass their tests. But what is at issue is more difficult to ascertain: the thought processes these students are learning. Are they acquiring critical, analytical skills, or at least more of these than their counterparts elsewhere in Nepal? Or are they, like students in other Nepalese elementary and secondary schools, simply memorizing what they read in books and are told in classes?

To answer this question, in 1974 I asked students in the Khumjung school to draw simple maps showing how to get from their houses to the school. I chose mapmaking as a simple example of constructing a scientific model, since a useful map requires both abstraction and a verifiable one-to-one relation with reality. The maps, then, are an elementary indication of the children's ability to render the physical world symbolically and to understand and use scientific concepts generally.

I collected twenty-eight maps drawn by Sherpa children in grades four, five, six, and seven (the highest grade in 1974) of the Khumjung school, as follows:

Grade	Students enrolled	Number of maps
Fourth	12	12
Fifth	10	8
Sixth	8	4
Seventh	5	4
TOTAL	35	28

These numbers are not large enough to be statistically manipulable. Although 80 percent of the students enrolled in these classes produced maps, high attrition at the time of my study resulted in the underrepresentation of the oldest and most advanced students.

Ascertaining student age was difficult. Most children in a single grade were approximately the same age, and those in lower grades were generally younger than those in higher grades, but a range of four or five years in a given grade is not unusual. Furthermore, although the children may be grouped to some extent according to ability, some of them may be in a given grade simply because of their parents' ability to spare them to attend school or because of their age when they began school. The issue is crucial: if all the ages are not known, it becomes difficult to decide whether the child's grade level or chronological age determines the type and the detail of a map.

Adult Sherpas are often aware of the day of the week they were born and the year of their twelve-year cycle (so one knows whether a child is, say, eight years old or twenty), but this information was not readily available for schoolchildren. I had genealogical information only for Khunde and Khumjung, and from this I determined the ages of fifteen of the children.

Arranging the maps according to the ascending ages of the children produces exactly the progression one would expect: the maps of the oldest students are clearly more abstract and maplike than those of the very youngest.

The maps of all but the youngest Sherpa children, however, are generally more sophisticated than similar maps drawn by Newar, Limbu, Chhetri, and Gurung children (see Dart and Pradhan 1967). Fura

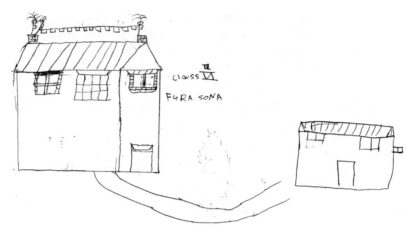

Fig. 52.   Map by Fura Sona, aged nine.

Sona's map (Fig. 52) is very much like the Limbu boy's map (Fig. 53), but Fura Sona, at nine, was the youngest of the Sherpas in my sample, whereas the Limbu map that hers resembles was by a boy of fifteen. Fura Sona's map shows her house and the school, with a short, undifferentiated path between them. Although a number of maps by older children also show their house and school on a single path, that path intersects and divides, turning and twisting along past recognizable landmarks, such as other houses or a temple.[3] Some of these maps dwell more on what is interesting about the village than on spatial relationships; but the maps' significance lies in their showing more than merely the house, the school, and a few landmarks. In them the children make some attempt to relate their way of getting to school to a larger geographical context.

The maps of seventh-grade children (Figs. 54–56) attempt to symbolize spatial relationships abstractly and clearly. All three maps not only show the house and school as recognizable buildings but keep them relatively small, much more nearly proportional to the distances involved. The number of landmarks increases, and everything is labeled so that a stranger looking at the map will understand its symbols. Where trail intersections might cause confusion, these older students are careful to put in the other trail. That correct choices must be made to arrive at the school, not somewhere else, is understood.

The lack of sophistication of all these maps compared with those by American children (Fig. 57) can be explained by cultural and environmental differences between the two groups. Sherpas are used to an en-

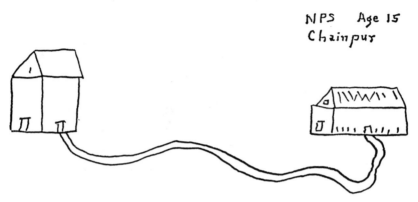

Fig. 53.   Map by a fifteen-year-old Limbu boy.

vironment of steep slopes with relatively few flat places and must there-fore handle spatial relationships in three, rather than only two, dimensions to construct an abstract and realistic spatial mode. To represent height on a two-dimensional surface is a challenging topographic problem. In a bird's-eye view of a steep slope (the usual perspective for Western spatial constructs like maps), two points may look close together although they are actually far apart—but on a vertical, not a horizontal, plane. The problem that Sherpa and most Nepalese children (and adults, for that matter) face is that faced by any mountain people explaining how far away a place is. A destination may be only half a mile away but up a steep and difficult slope. Therefore, as any trekker in Nepal knows, distance is measured in time, not linear units.

The Sherpa children thus tend to construct their maps to show the relation of higher and lower, sacrificing that of depth and width, so that the map represents a vertical cross section rather than a bird's-eye view. The difficulty is that horizontal relations are important as well, but once the mapmaker has emphasized the vertical, it is almost impossible to show horizontal relations as well. One of the older students, Ang Kami, tried to realize all three dimensions at once (see Fig. 54), but on a two-dimensional surface, a one-to-one correspondence is difficult to establish; Ang Kami's buildings thus tilt at weird angles, and perspective is lost. The only map that would really work for Sherpas would be a topographical map with contour lines to mark elevation—an abstraction so remote from the way Sherpas see their world that they do not use it. Indeed few Westerners can read, let alone construct, a topographic map.

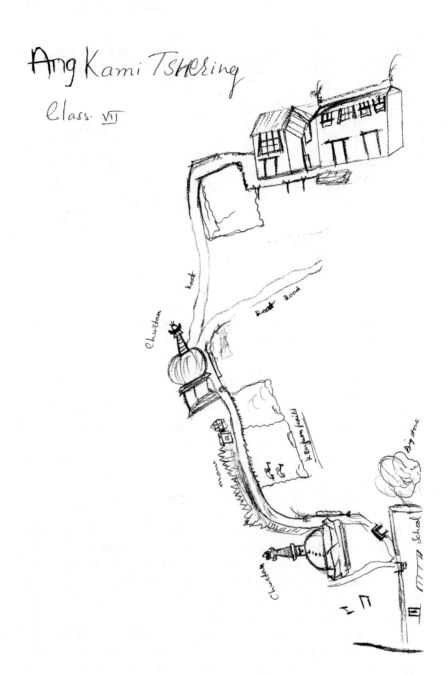

Fig. 54. Map by Ang Kami Tsering.

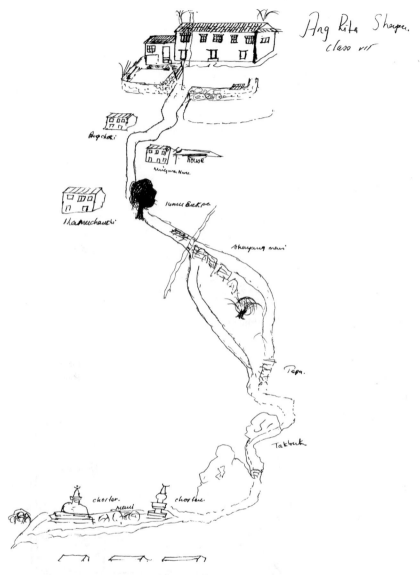

Fig. 55.   Map by Ang Rita Sherpa.

Conceptualizing spatial relations is also difficult for Sherpas because their environment does not present them with obvious geometrical reference points. American children generally live in an environment whose grid is arranged and labeled for them in a system of Cartesian coordinates, with many wide streets intersecting at right angles; the

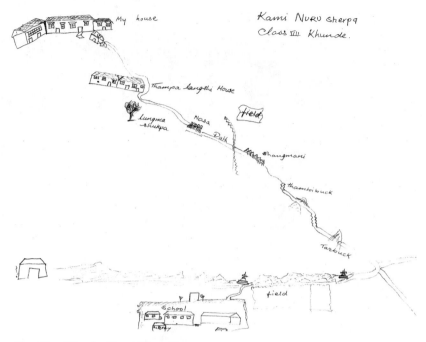

Kami Nuru sherpa
Class VII Khunde.

My house

Thampa langahi House

Lungma bhukpa

Nasa

Path

field

Shangmani

thamboibuck

Tarbuck

School

Library

field

Fig. 56. Map by Kami Nuru Sherpa.

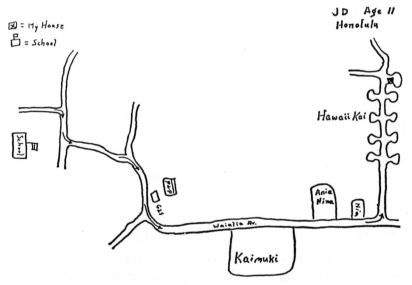

☒ = My House
⌂ = School

JD   Age 11
Honolulu

Hawaii Kai

School

field

Gas

Ania
Nima

Nia

Waialia Av.

Kaimuki

Fig. 57. Map by an eleven-year-old American boy.

Sherpas' environment is much more random and, by accepted town-planning conventions, chaotic. Most American children know that getting to school requires walking a certain number of blocks, then making a ninety-degree turn left or right, walking another set number of blocks, and so on. The Sherpas have no such reference system. It seems logical, then, that Sherpas see directions as a process rather than as a series of spatial relationships, especially when most of their trails are narrow, winding affairs; there is a path where the going is easiest, where nature permits it, not where a civil engineer with bulldozers at his disposal has dictated it.

Finally, American children learn early and systematically how to read maps and make diagrams. It is then no wonder that American children's maps are "better" than those of the Sherpas. Although Sherpas have maps of their entire country in their classrooms, they have never seen anything like a city map. To ask American children to draw a map is to ask them to do the routine; to ask Sherpa children to draw a map is to ask them to apply themselves creatively to the unfamiliar.

The Sherpa schoolchildren's maps show that they have acquired, by Nepalese standards, an above-average ability to conceive and project abstract spatial relationships. Measured by this cognitive dimension, the schools work.

INCULCATION OF VALUES

Another measure of what the schools are doing, apart from the knowledge and thinking skills they teach, lies in the values they inculcate. To determine the relative strength of various values, I asked the Khumjung schoolchildren to rank fourteen different occupations or activities they might follow after they had finished their studies (Table 2). The table shows that the values are distributed over a broad spectrum, but clearly there are patterns. The most-desired goals are helping one's parents and becoming educated, whereas having children is the least desired. The responses largely reflect the goals of young children who have not yet considered their postschool plans, and to that extent they are not particularly realistic. In fact, many of the children eventually do the most practical thing: they work for tourists.

It is not surprising that the most popular choices were to help parents and to be educated. Even though Sherpas in later life sometimes let their parents fend for themselves, Sherpa children are taught to be help-

TABLE 2   KHUMJUNG SCHOOLCHILDREN'S
            POST-SCHOOL GOALS

Goal[a]	Number of children ranking each goal[b]													
	1	2	3	4	5	6	7	8	9	10	11	12	13	14
Help parents	10	3	2	3	2	2	0	0	1	0	1	0	0	0
Teach	0	4	1	1	3	0	4	0	4	3	1	1	1	0
Work for village welfare	1	2	4	1	3	2	2	4	1	1	2	0	0	1
Work hard	0	1	0	1	1	2	2	3	3	1	0	3	6	1
Be rich	0	1	3	2	4	2	1	0	1	1	2	4	1	0
Work with tourists	2	0	0	2	3	3	3	1	2	2	2	3	3	1
Live in Kathmandu	0	2	0	0	2	0	2	3	0	3	3	3	3	3
Work for religion	1	2	2	2	1	2	1	2	4	3	2	0	0	1
Be a doctor	0	1	4	0	2	3	0	1	2	4	2	0	2	1
Be independent	1	4	3	2	0	2	3	0	2	2	1	1	1	0
Be famous	0	0	0	5	2	2	2	2	2	2	5	2	0	1
Help the nation	2	2	5	2	0	2	2	3	1	1	0	2	2	0
Get more education	7	1	0	2	1	2	2	3	0	1	2	1	1	1
Have many children	0	1	0	0	0	0	0	1	1	0	1	5	3	12

[a]The fourteen goals are listed in order from most valued (top of list) to least.

[b]Columns read from left (most valued) to right (least valued). Because some of the twenty-four children surveyed did not rank all the goals listed, in a few cases (i.e., columns under 4, 13, and 14) the number of responses does not add up to twenty-four.

ful. Similarly, schoolchildren are told that education is important, and their attendance at school predisposes them to believe it. Hence it is not surprising that education is ranked high.

Both of the top-ranked goals imply a respect for authority figures (teachers and parents) that is congruent with Sherpa culture; hence the schools reinforce it. Similar values emerged when the same twenty-four Khumjung students were asked to rank five distinguished persons (Table 3). In this case the choices given do not realistically allow for losers; Sherpas respect all these persons. Thus the good sardar places fifth not because he doesn't command respect but because he is the only person who is not a virtual demigod. All the others are powerful individuals who by virtue of their uniqueness cannot be emulated but only admired, respected, and, whenever possible, propitiated. They are persons of learning (including religious learning) or great largesse, and all are figures of vast authority.

What is striking in Tables 2 and 3 is the discontinuity between the ideal and the actual. In neither table does working for tourists or being a sardar (what most students eventually do) rank high. Although the desire to be a sardar is realistic and the profession itself admirable, the

TABLE 3   KHUMJUNG SCHOOLCHILDREN'S RANKING
           OF PERSONS

	Order of ranking (by 24 children)				
	First	Second	Third	Fourth	Fifth
King of Nepal	10	7	4	2	1
Dalai Lama	10	6	2	2	4
Sir Edmund Hillary	3	7	7	6	1
Tengboche rimpoche	0	4	10	6	4
Good sardar	1	0	1	8	14

status of the sardar can never match that of the king of Nepal or the Dalai Lama.

The two most highly respected individuals, moreover, represent two entirely different traditions; one is the venerated Buddhist leader, the other the ultimate political leader of the Hindu nation, both accepted as reincarnations and both admired for their overwhelming power, sanctity, and charisma. It is no coincidence that many Sherpas wear two picture buttons on their shirts and blouses: one of the king of Nepal, the other of the Dalai Lama (Fig. 58).

MONASTIC CONTRASTS

It would be an oversimplification to portray the schools as the only outside educational institution to be recently imported to Khumbu. High above the trail along the Bhote Koshi, about halfway between Namche Bazaar and Thame, lies a small monastic establishment built around 1970 at the hamlet of Laudo. The Laudo *gompa* is a seasonal arm of the much larger Kopan Monastery near Boudhanath in the Kathmandu Valley. In the mid-1970s when I visited Kopan, it was patronized not only by traditional Tibetan Buddhists but also by a large European and American population, whose financial contributions enabled the monastery to carry on a vigorous program of meditation and instruction in Buddhist philosophy and practice. Its principal leadership was in the hands of two lamas, one a *tulku* (reincarnated lama); both spoke excellent English and possessed a remarkable ability to present their teachings in an easily comprehensible manner to those who were foreign to the whole tradition they represented (Fig. 59).

At Laudo in summer a dozen or so young *thawas*, mostly from the

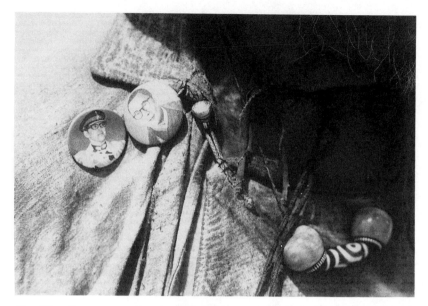

Fig. 58. Sherpas regard political loyalty to the king and religious loyalty to the Dalai Lama as completely compatible.

Thame area (but including an Australian child), pursue the standard monastic scholarly routine. The older European clientele does not take part in this summer operation (though by the 1980s most of the Laudo summer population was European). In the winter the young *thawas* descend again to Kathmandu to continue their studies.

The monastic studies of the young Kopan *thawas* were similar to those at Tengboche, although otherwise there was no connection between them and the monasteries in Tengboche and Thame. To determine whether the Kopan *thawas* were developing along lines similar to those of their counterparts in Tengboche and the village schools, I administered a modified "respected person" test to six of the Kopan *thawas*. But I asked them to rank not only the five figures I had asked the others to rank but also a sixth person, their own reincarnate lama, the Laudo rimpoche (Table 4).

The results of this test differ from those of the tests administered to the Khumjung schoolchildren.[4] The top three Kopan choices overwhelmingly favored one of the three lamas listed, although Sir Edmund Hillary was chosen twice as second choice and once as third choice. The Kopan choices agree with those of the Khumjung children, however, in the low ranking of a good sardar. Five of the six respondents

Fig. 59. The guiding forces behind Kopan, a monastery that has attracted many Western Buddhists. Sherpas believe that the geshe, at left, after his death, was reincarnated in a Spanish boy in 1987, the first time a lama had been reincarnated in a European.

ranked that person lowest. The most striking difference is the place accorded the king of Nepal, whom none of the *thawas* ranked in the top three positions. Although the schoolchildren ranked him in a first-place tie with the Dalai Lama, the Kopan *thawas* ranked him above only the sardar.

It is clear that the political enculturation the children experience in the schools is powerful and effective. The Kopan *thawas,* as part of a monastery with no connection to either the Nepalese national educational system or traditional Nepalese Buddhist monasteries, have no interest in, or possibly even much knowledge of, the Hindu monarch who rules their country. The reasons are obvious: the Kopan institution is relatively new and financed largely by foreign sources. Therefore it

TABLE 4   KOPAN *THAWAS*' RANKING OF PERSONS

	Order of ranking (by 6 *thawas*)					
	First	*Second*	*Third*	*Fourth*	*Fifth*	*Sixth*
King of Nepal	0	0	0	2	3	1
Dalai Lama	4	1	1	0	0	0
Tengboche rimpoche	1	1	3	1	0	0
Laudo rimpoche	1	2	1	2	0	0
Good sardar	0	0	0	0	1	5
Sir Edmund Hillary	0	2	1	1	2	0

has little connection with other Nepalese institutions, either political or religious.

The independence of the Kopan group has enabled it to flourish in a way that Tengboche has not. Since the monastery does not fall under the Nepalese educational system, the Kopan lamas are free to conduct their school as they wish. Their enrollments are high for good reasons. First, they waive or reduce the modest monthly fee for those *thawas* who cannot pay the full amount. Until recently, when a hostel was constructed, *thawas* at Tengboche had to arrange even their own housing (the monks' houses are all privately owned). Second, they teach a wide variety of subjects, Tibetan and modern, including English. Third, at Kopan instruction is organized in a regular class setting, whereas at Tengboche each monk studies by himself in his own quarters. In Tibet, the organized teaching of monks was offered at different levels, but such instruction—including the classic Tibetan monastic disputations—has traditionally not been available at Tengboche for want of the personnel to offer it.

Enrollments at Tengboche have greatly improved in recent years. One group of fourteen *thawas* has been inducted into *chhowa,* the stage at which those with some education who can recite the regular ritual performances of the monastery join the older *thawas* (now about fifteen in number) in the main row. Of the fourteen, eight pursued higher religious studies near Boudhanath in Kathmandu, sponsored by two prospering trekking company managers: Kalden Sherpa, originally from Khumjung and the first Khumbu Sherpa to be educated in Kathmandu (see p. 69), and Stan Armington, an American. In addition to these a new group of twenty or so is accommodated at the new hostel at Tengboche. They pay Rs 200 per month for food. By 1989 there were about twenty-five monks and twenty-five students resident at Tengboche.

Plate 1.   Sherpas live in permanent villages only part of the year. In the summer they move with their animals to higher pastures, such as Gokyo (a Khumjung *yersa*, "summer settlement"), between the lake and the off-white ribbon of the Lungsampa Glacier. The black peak in the background is Everest.

Plate 2. A girl looks after her little brother near Gokyo.

Plates 3 and 4. *Above:* Every Saturday morning shoppers from all the Khumbu villages crowd the weekly bazaar at Namche. *Below:* During the rest of the week the Namche shops remain open for business.

Plate 5. A tourist and a monk examine a wicker basket full of grain. Wearing only thin cotton clothes in the cold morning air, the seller is eager to sell his merchandise as soon as possible and return to warmer weather at lower altitudes.

Plates 6 and 7. *Above:* Participants in a town meeting in Khumjung discuss ways to ensure that Sherpa land is properly registered so that it cannot be claimed by the government. The presence of the Tengboche rimpoche (*seated at far left*) lends legitimacy to the meeting. The speaker, in the red sweater, is a Nepalese veterinarian stationed in Namche to help run the government yak farm. *Below:* An attendance book is kept at the meeting to prove that a sufficient number of people were present to legitimize the proceedings. Here an illiterate woman presses her thumb to an inkpad to make a thumbprint beside her name.

Plate 8. Ang Tsering, a climbing Sherpa and the mayor of the Khumjung Panchayat (village council), addresses the meeting.

Plate 9. The fortunes and influence of the Khunde Major, a tax collector (*pembu*), have declined markedly in recent years as leadership has passed to the younger generation from the elders.

Plate 10. Former elders still speak up, including Konjo Chumbi, who once traveled around the world showing a yeti scalp to scientists.

Plate 11. Wangchu Lama, another former elder, makes the humorous point that whereas traditionally Sherpas have done everything they could to keep the government from knowing what was going on, now they are going out of their way to be sure the government knows that their land belongs to them.

Plate 12.   Trekkers set up tents in front of Tengboche Monastery. One of the trekking lodges in the background is operated by the national park, one by the monastery, and one by a private concern.

Plate 13. The annual Mani-Rimdu festival draws Sherpas from all over Khumbu.

Plates 14, 15, and 16. The famous painter Kappa Kalden, who before his death in 1984 was responsible for most of the religious art in Khumbu, including the paintings on the interior walls of Tengboche Monastery. He had also done the art work for Rongbuk Monastery on the northern side of Everest, in Tibet. By the 1970s he had added a modern, impressionistic style to his repertoire and spent most of his time turning out paintings for tourists. One of his paintings was chosen to represent Nepal in the UNICEF calendar for 1972. Two of his four sons became painters too. One son, Ang Pemma, works for a trekking agency as a cook and cooked for me during much of the time I was collecting information for this book. The youngest son, Ang Rita, tells his own story in chapter 3 (see pp. 98–105).

Plate 17. Because of the monopoly on trade with Tibet over the Nangpa La granted them by the Nepalese government in the nineteenth century, some Namche traders, such as Ang Tsering, accumulated great wealth.

Plate 18.   Mingma Tsering and Ang Doli in formal attire, with Ang Rita.

Plate 19.   Two first-graders in Thame adopt the traditional respectful *namaste* posture to sing the Nepalese national anthem before morning classes.

The Laudo *gompa* draws a number of young local boys (mostly from the Thame Valley) as *thawas,* and many of these move on, after three or four years, to the established *gompas* at Tengboche and Thame. In this way they acquire the rudiments of English and Nepali before they enter the older, traditional monasteries.

PAST, PRESENT, AND FUTURE

A final way to assess the effect of the schools on the outlook of the Sherpa students is to examine the students' view of themselves now, in the past, and in the future. To do this I used a modified version of the Cantril Self-Anchoring test.[5] This test consists of a picture of a ladder with ten rungs on which I asked the children to place themselves where they felt they were at the present, using the letter A to denote this position; then to indicate where they were five years before with the letter B; and finally to place themselves where they expected to be five years in the future, using the letter C. After marking the appropriate rungs, they wrote a short essay about each position. The logic of this test is that it allows a person to estimate his or her own life chances, to describe the content of these chances, and to indicate what sort of hope and momentum there is to the trajectory of their lives in the near future. Since I administered the test to nineteen Khumjung schoolchildren as well as to three *thawas* in Tengboche Monastery, it is possible to compare what happens to values through education. This test has the advantage of inquiring both about what has actually happened and what the person realistically expects to happen.

Almost all the Khumjung schoolchildren respondents viewed the future more positively than they did either the present or the past. In the future the children primarily want to make money, work with tourists, become teachers or doctors, or work for the welfare and development of their village. They commonly described the past as a time when they knew very little (could not read or write, for instance) and were unable to work in any capacity. Thus the past is a time of unfulfilled potential and the future a time when energies and talents will be productively engaged one way or another.

As would be expected, the older, seventh grade, students were more articulate about all three positions than those in the lower grades. Their plans for the future were more specific and reflected an aroused social conscience. One student wanted to be a teacher but would settle for working with tourists. Another said he would give his money to his parents but also spoke of becoming responsible, starting his own household, and working with tourists. He emphasized running a clean and healthy home. The emphasis on work, the household, and the village community does not duplicate but overlaps that in the fourteen-goal value test. The values revealed in both tests are consonant with traditional Sherpa culture.

Three *thawas* studying at Tengboche were also given the Cantril test. Like the Khumjung children, all three *thawas* viewed the future as the high point of their lives, but for an entirely different reason: in the future they would become lamas and be able to devote their lives completely to religion. All three, like the students generally, rated the past lowest on the ladder. Their essays implied that in the past they had felt pessimistic about becoming lamas, but now they were more hopeful. Generally the positions and overall optimism about life chances were similar for the schoolchildren and *thawas;* only the specific future careers differed. Despite the somewhat arbitrary way parents "assign" children to either a school or monastery,[6] students in each are happy with their fate.

CASE STUDIES

The ultimate measure of how the schools change Sherpa life is the subsequent experience of individuals who have gone through the system. Capsule life histories of the first graduates of the Khumjung school, who in 1966 finished what was then the highest grade, the fifth, show how fundamentally life chances have been altered.

Mingma Norbu (Fig. 60) attended secondary schools in Amp Pipal and Ananda Kuti and after his Intermediate Science degree (I.Sc.) won a four-year scholarship to Lincoln College in Christ Church, New Zealand, where he received a diploma in national parks and recreation. He worked for two years as the warden of Sagarmatha National Park, then spent two years earning a master of science in national resource management at the University of Manitoba, Canada. He now works for the King Mahendra Trust and in 1986 coauthored a report on the feasibility of establishing a conservation area—a new concept in Nepal—in the Annapurna region. He lives in both Khumjung and Kathmandu, depending on his schedule of work and study. He is married to a Khumjung Sherpani and has two children.

Lhakpa Norbu attended secondary schools in Amp Pipal and Ananda Kuti. After his older brother, with whom he shared a wife in a poly-

Fig. 60. Mingma Norbu, son-in-law of Ang Tsering (see Figs. 103 and 104), at his desk in the National Parks office in Kathmandu.

androus marriage, died in a mountaineering accident, Lhakpa Norbu was forced to leave school and return home to take care of his family. He taught in the Khumjung school for two years and for the last eight years has been a trek leader (above the sardar level) for Mt. Travel. He is now the *pradhan panch* (mayor) of the Khumjung Panchayat. He lives in Khumjung with his wife and six children, five his brother's and one his own.

Lhakpa Thundu attended secondary school in the Solu-Khumbu district capital of Saleri for four years before he was suspended for participating in a student strike. He was charged with throwing rocks at the king's picture but was later acquitted. He was not allowed to take the S.L.C. exam. He worked as sardar for Mt. Travel for ten years and for Himalayan Journeys for one year. He is chairman of the youth organization in Khumjung, where he lives with his wife, also from Khumjung, and their four children.

Pasang Tsering attended secondary school in Saleri for four years and after passing his S.L.C. exam taught for two years in Khumjung. He has worked for Mt. Travel for twelve years, where he is an "A" sardar (the highest of three grades). He lives with his wife, a Khunde native, in Khunde.

Ang Tsering did his S.L.C. exam from Saleri. After receiving his I.Sc., he attended medical school in Darbanga, India, on a Remote Areas Scholarship provided by His Majesty's Government. He returned without finishing his degree to work for two years for Rover Trek, which is owned by his brother-in-law. He married a Belgian woman and six years ago founded Asian Trekking, which has a near monopoly on Belgian trekking groups. By the rule of ultimogeniture, Ang Tsering's youngest brother inherited his parents' house in Khumjung. Ang Tsering himself lives in Kathmandu most of the year but frequently spends summers in Belgium.

Ang Phu, after completing the fifth grade, went to work for Mt. Travel. He climbed Everest twice and was the first to reach the summit by two different routes. He died during his second descent (on the west ridge), on a Yugoslavian expedition.

Pertemba (Fig. 61) did not continue beyond fifth grade. He came to Kathmandu in 1966 to work for Nepal's first trekking agency, Mt. Travel, which had just been founded by Col. Jimmy Roberts. While working for Mt. Travel, Pertemba also managed to join a number of mountaineering expeditions, first as a high-altitude porter, later as a sardar, and finally as the coleader of the American expedition that made the first ascent of Gaurishanker. He has given climbing seminars in Europe and the United States and has climbed Mt. Everest three times. In 1985 he left Mt. Travel and with two business partners— another Sherpa and a Chhetri—founded a new trekking agency, Nepal Himal. He lives in Kathmandu with his Namche Sherpani wife and children but also retains his house in Khumjung.

Finally, to provide one biography in greater depth, Ang Rita (no relation to Mingma Tsering's son, Ang Rita, introduced in chapter 1) tells his own story:

Mt. Everest was conquered in 1953 by Sherpa Tenzing and Edmund Hillary, and I was born in that same year in Khumjung village; my father was Kappa Kalden, a famous painter. The conquest of Everest has proved a special reward to me, as I with my contemporaries got the opportunity to be in the first class to go to the first school built by the hero of Everest, Sir Edmund Hillary. He built this school in 1961 in my village, Khumjung, as a result of his appreciation and affection for the Sherpa people.

The ready-made aluminum school building was about to be assembled in Khumjung by New Zealand builders. Mr. Tem Dorje Sherpa, a widely experienced teacher from Darjeeling, was already in Khumjung, making house visits

Fig. 61. Pertemba at work in his newly founded trekking agency, Nepal Himal.

to meet the parents and encourage them to send their children to school, as none of the parents knew anything about education at that time. As far as I could understand, my parents were rather conservative, and I was quite worried about whether my parents, especially my father, would agree to send any of their children to school. My eleven-year-old brother and I, who was nine, were the most likely candidates to enroll, as my other brothers and sisters were a little too old to start schooling.

The next worry that pursued me was even if my father agreed to send one of us to school, which one of the two of us would he send? Traditionally Sherpa parents tend to favor the youngest son of the family, since this son will be responsible to look after the parents in their old age, as well as to look after all their social and religious activities in the future. This social norm applied very well to me, since when the teacher called on my father one evening,

I heard my father replying, "I want to send my youngest son to school." It was a moment of great elation for me, but of course it was disappointing for my brother, who might have had an equal desire for education.

When negotiations between parents and the teacher finished, classes began in the open grass field near where the school building was being installed. I have a vivid memory of how the teacher started. He introduced the Nepali alphabet to us by asking us to draw a Sherpa house pillar, which is shaped like an English T. Then he asked us to draw around this pillar, thus completing the first letter of the Nepali alphabet, क . This letter is pronounced "ka," and, coincidentally, the Sherpa word for the house pillar is pronounced almost the same, "kā." [7] Those who could draw that ka felt very proud and excited.

Day after day became more and more exciting as we kept learning more. In a year's time I was able to read and write basic Nepali and had some knowledge of mathematics and English. At first my favorite subject was English, and I would even, for example, write letters to the teacher at Pangboche in English, just for practice. At that time I was very impressed with the English spoken by a Khumjung Sherpa who had served for about ten years in the Indian army. He sounded very fluent, but later I realized that his English was very broken and full of mistakes, whereas the English I was learning was correct. Later, when I realized that I wanted to become a medical doctor, I got more interested in science. I proudly used to read my lessons very loudly at home so that my parents would be happy to see my progress. [8]

As I mentioned above, none of the parents in Khumjung had any knowledge of education, and none of them knew how long it might take to educate their children. My parents envisaged that everything would be learned in two years' time. So during these two years my studies proceeded quite smoothly, without much interference from domestic tasks, though I used to volunteer in the mornings and evenings to help with all the seasonal tasks of the house, such as carrying manure to the fields, collecting fodder for livestock, collecting firewood, etc.

But when my schooling was prolonged beyond what my parents had envisaged, I encountered completely different attitudes from my parents. They became quite harsh about my continuing in school and put increased pressure on me to become more involved in housework rather than encouraging me to go on with schooling. Sometimes this made me feel disappointed, but I tried to persevere without getting too disheartened from this kind of problem. I used to work very hard in the mornings and evenings to compensate for the loss of time while I was in school. In this way I continued for the third, fourth, and fifth grades.

I noticed that every year some of my friends, either in my class or from younger ones, had to drop out because of circumstances similar to those I was struggling with. Most cases of dropping out were caused by long periods of absence from classes due to parental pressure to look after harvesting or livestock in summer settlements at higher elevations, several days' walk from home. These responsibilities required longer periods of involvement, and when you cannot then catch up on the lost lessons, you get frustrated and finally feel impelled to drop altogether.

I started the first grade in 1961 and finished after grade five, as Khumjung was only a primary school at that time. During this five-year period I used to top the class in all examinations, and this was a factor in my selection for one of three scholarships, sponsored by Robert Kennedy through the United Mission to Nepal, to attend high school in Amp Pipal, near Gorkha, in west Nepal. Thus my struggle and perseverance paid off. After leaving Khumjung, I did not have such domestic problems any more (my parents did not object to my going away for further schooling), and my study went more smoothly for the next several years.

To take up this scholarship, I along with my two other colleagues from Khumjung School took our first airplane flight, from Lukla to Kathmandu, where we contacted the mission headquarters. They had arranged a flight for us to go to Amp Pipal, where I experienced a sharp contrast from what I was used to, both in culture and many other aspects. I lived in a small, tin-roofed hostel with no windows; there were a few rooms and a common kitchen. There was no electricity, so I always studied in the dim light of a kerosene lamp. We boys shared all the responsibilities at the hostel, including cooking. I used to study so much, as I had at Khumjung, that I would cook with one hand and hold a book in the other in the smoke-filled kitchen shared by all the boys. So in 1966 I enrolled in class six in Amp Pipal and finished class eight in 1967. I finished three grades in two years, because after the semi-annual examinations during class six I was promoted to class seven.

During these two years we were encouraged to go to church every Sunday and get involved in all the missionary activities, which I admit were enjoyable. We learned many hymns, in both Nepali and English. One of my favorites was "Give Me Oil in My Lamp, Keep It Burning, Burning, Burning." Our obligation toward the missionaries grew because of their financial support for our educations as well as the friendship they extended for two years, and eventually my two friends and I sensed a kind of threat to our own Buddhist religion. When we informed Sir Edmund Hillary about the situation, he generously made arrangements to transfer us from Amp Pipal to Ananda Kuti, a Buddhist boarding school behind Swayambunath in Kathmandu. But neither there nor anywhere else was I ever treated differently, by Nepalese or foreigners, because of my caste or religion.

Ananda Kuti brought many changes in my life: change in the mode of living, from a village to a town, from a thatch-roof school to a modern school building, from a kerosene lamp to electric lights, from a calm and quiet place to a busy, noisy place. I continued to study hard, but I also took time to read newspapers and magazines, visit the school library, and play games, particularly volleyball, football, and badminton. I also took part in scouting and excursions organized by the school. All this acquainted me with the world on a broader scale. I did not have the feeling that everything was so complex, as I had felt at Amp Pipal, because by this time the development of my language skills had removed that feeling.

I enrolled in class nine at Ananda Kuti in 1968 and finished my School Leaving Certificate examination in 1969 at the top of the list of 19,000 students from all over Nepal who took the S.L.C. that year. This success elated Sir Edmund and all my Sherpa fellows. Sir Edmund agreed to finance my further study in premedical science, as I had a strong desire to become a Sherpa doctor and work in one of the hospitals in Solu-Khumbu built by the foundation Sir Edmund had established, now called the Himalayan Trust.

In 1970 I enrolled in Amrit Science College and finished my Intermediate Science degree in 1973. In 1971 Sir Edmund arranged for me to visit Chicago briefly to attend a Himalayan Trust fund-raising meeting. I gave an eight-minute speech to more than 2,500 people, describing Sherpa life and the changes brought by the schools they were supporting. This was my first visit abroad, and it was really a great time for me.

After completing my I.Sc., my first option was to go to a medical college in India, because of the many similar aspects between India and Nepal. But this had become impossible because my age exceeded the age limit for this scholarship, and this forced me to take a medical scholarship offered by the Burmese government. So in 1974 two Nepali colleagues and I went to study medicine in Rangoon. About five months after our arrival, student riots erupted all over the country on an issue related to the death of U Thant, a Burmese national who had been the U.N. General Secretary. The students felt that the military government had not accorded U Thant proper respect when his body was returned to Burma, so they rioted. Because of the riots the government closed down all the universities and arranged for us to return to Nepal until they reopened.

So we came back to Nepal in 1975, when the Himalayan Trust was starting to build a hospital at Phaplu, in Solu [Fig. 62]. I joined the construction team, but I worked mainly helping the doctor who had begun to treat local people from his tent. I spent about six months at Phaplu and then received a message that we should go back to Burma. We again shuttled to Rangoon and started our usual classes. But after no more than five months, unrest developed again, forcing the government to close down the universities a second time. We were again sent back to Nepal, and this time we decided that whatever happened in Burma, we would not return there but stay in Nepal. We were just too fed up to go back. I enrolled in a public administration course at Tribhuvan University for two years and received my B.A. in 1976.

While working in Phaplu I met Ang Zangmu, and the following year we got married. I soon became a father of my first girl, Phurba Yanjin. After completing my degree, I got a job in Trans-Himalayan Trekking in 1978, where I worked until 1985. During this period we had two more children: our second daughter, Tsering, and a son, Pemba Tsering. We settled down more or less permanently in Kathmandu, though we visited Khumjung to see my aged father sometimes during the monsoon [Fig. 63]. After my father died in 1984, we did not have much chance to go to Khumjung, but I still keep the family house there. My sister takes care of it.

During my seven years of working with Trans-Himalayan Trekking I was quite satisfied with the prosperity that came from earning a good income, etc. But I was not satisfied with my social identity, as the pride I felt from being a better-educated person made me feel that I should be doing something better and different from what other Sherpas were doing. While this urge was growing stronger, Sir Edmund Hillary nominated me for a project organized by the

Fig. 62. Some Solu families, like the owners of this house—virtually a mansion—in the village of Phaplu, are very wealthy. The house, which is surrounded by a stone wall and has an attached kitchen, is without parallel in Khumbu. Two of the four sons of the house married American Peace Corps volunteers. An airstrip and a hotel, in addition to the hospital Ang Rita mentions, were built in Phaplu during the 1970s.

Himalayan Trust and the Sheraton Hotel, the object of which was to train young Sherpas in hotel management. Man by nature always sees greener grass on the other side of the fence, and so I accepted this opportunity. In 1986 I went for a year's training in the Everest Sheraton Hotel in Kathmandu. I should frankly admit that this one year was a hard one for me, as my health and the nature of the work, involving long hours of both day and night duty, did not go well together. Then Sir Edmund Hillary invited me to work for the Himalayan Trust at an executive level, and I accepted that job in 1987. I have been working there ever since.

I now work in the trust office in Kathmandu, where my main responsibilities are looking after many scholarship students enrolled in the various college

Fig. 63.   Ang Rita with his wife, two of his three children, and the baby son of his wife's sister, who lives with her husband in New York. He built this house on the northern edge of Kathmandu and then rented it out while he in turn rented a smaller apartment in another home. He moved into this house in 1988. (By the rule of ultimogeniture, he inherited his parents' house in Khumjung, which now stands empty most of the time.)

campuses, managing supplies and their transport to hospitals and schools in Solu-Khumbu, coordinating arrangements with HMG officials, organizing construction materials for new projects, etc. In the fall of 1988 I spent a month in England in a fund-raising program with British Venture Scouts.

At present, I have the additional responsibility of helping to organize the rebuilding of Tengboche Monastery, which burned to the ground on January 19, 1989, in a fire caused by the new electricity. My involvement in this work stems mainly from the commitment the Himalayan Trust has made for a large share of the rebuilding costs. Also, I have been elected as secretary of the executive committee that we Sherpas have formed to look after the reconstruction of the monastery.

There are many things I miss about Khumbu, particularly my relatives there and the good climate. I also miss our festivals. We do celebrate Sherpa festivals in Kathmandu too, but it's not quite the same thing. Of course there are also problems living in Khumbu—difficulties getting water and firewood, for example. Also, life has changed somewhat with all the tourists. Earlier, we felt we should extend our hospitality to foreigners, without receiving any payment. But now that there are so many foreigners, we have become less hospitable and charge for firewood and food, for example. Overall I think I would rather live in Khumbu, but it is not possible to keep the job I have and live there.

My children all understand Sherpa, but when I speak it to them, they usually reply in Nepali. Sometimes they speak Sherpa for fun. It's our fault that they don't know more Sherpa, because we don't insist, as we should, that they learn it. I regret that sometimes. But there is still enough time for them to get back to the Sherpa language.

In their histories, these first graduates exemplify and even surpass the goals ranked highest in Table 2. The surviving graduates are almost all highly educated and work productively for the development of their village or country in various ways. Many of them have become moderately wealthy by traditional standards, but even those who spend most of their time in Kathmandu maintain strong ties with other Sherpas in Kathmandu and in Khumbu and contribute to village and monastic welfare.

Clearly, none of those who went on for further study could have made the choices they did or reached the levels they have attained without the education that started in their own village school. In that sense the schools have produced change: a generation of Sherpas is now following, in addition to their traditional Sherpa civic and religious life, a set of entirely new occupations earlier generations could scarcely have imagined.

Their accomplishments stand out when compared with those of their classmates who entered first grade with them but dropped out before fifth grade. The achievements of only three of the sixteen who left school match those of the graduates: two are sardars and the third owns a prosperous Namche hotel. Of the remaining thirteen, three are cretins, two are homemakers (only two girls enrolled the first year), two free-lance for trekking companies (a relatively undesirable job in the tourist industry), one herds yak, one farms, one works in a Kathmandu hotel, one worked in the Hotel Everest-View, one disappeared in India, one is unknown. Three died, none in mountaineering accidents.

The contrast with those in the same cohort in Khumjung or Khunde who never attended school at all is even more dramatic. Of the twenty-four in this category, fifteen are women. Except for one who weaves carpets in Kathmandu, they are all now Khumbu homemakers. They never attended school either because they were girls, or because their families were poor, or for both reasons (some were poor but had brothers who did go to school). Of the nine boys, two became monks (one still is a monk), four were cretins, and three, like many of the others in this group, were too poor to go to school. Of the three, two have non-sardar trekking jobs. Two of the twenty-four have died, neither in a mountaineering accident.

CONCLUSION

The changes brought about by these schools have depended on the cultural makeup of the communities in which they are set and on the position of the schools in the multiple society of which they are a part; on the presence of indigenous educational institutions; on the type of teacher employed; on the conception of knowledge; on the curriculum content and values taught; and on the traditional ideal of the educated person.

The individuating religion of the Sherpas (Sherpas attempt to increase their store of merit to improve their chances for a better reincarnation in the next life) is counterbalanced by the civic hierarchy described in chapter 2 and a concomitant civic pride. In their social organization (nuclear family, "love" as opposed to "arranged" marriages, generally equal rights of husband and wife), their community government and organization (democratic, with leadership roles determined by individual achievement), and their values and view of the good life (emphasizing flexibility, achievement, concern for the wider society), the Sherpas are generically different from Westerners yet are more like them than are their Hindu countrymen.[9] These features underlie and are reinforced by the sophisticated attitudes that have come with large-scale trading expeditions to cosmopolitan cities. After decades of contact with mountaineering expeditions, the Sherpas have become familiar with Western ways of doing things and ideas of adventure and innovation. Thus the Sherpas constitute a specific example of "groups inhabiting rural areas which are more Westernized in their style of life than many urban groups" (Srinivas 1966, 48).

When a rural social and cultural system (that of Buddhist Sherpas) is more democratic, achievement oriented, and responsive to change than that represented by the dominant community (that of high Hindu castes) in the multiple-society continuum, the tacit assumption that the national educational system has nothing to offer rural minority cultures but modernity, as defined by the Hindu state, is false.

A Torrent of Tourists

To travel for economic or religious reasons—to pilgrimage sites, for example—is as ancient as any human activity. South Asia has for aeons had its own version of tourism: the Nepali term is *tirtha;* the word means "pilgrimage" but connotes an activity organized and commercialized enough to evoke reverberations of tourism in the modern sense. According to the *Bengal District Gazetteer,*

Most of the pilgrims who come to Puri form part of an organized tour, and nothing has stimulated pilgrimage so much as the organized system of pilgrim guides. The Pandas and Pariharis of the temple have divided among themselves the whole of India, each having an allotted circle, in which they claim to possess a monopoly of pilgrims. Two or three months before the beginning of the principal festivals, the Dola and Rath Jatras, they engage agents, mostly Brahmans and sometimes barbers and Gauras, and depute them to different parts of India in order to recruit pilgrims. These agents, known as batuwas (journeymen) in Oriya and sethos in Bengali, travel among the chief towns and villages in their circle, carrying with them nirmalya (half-boiled rice) offered to Jagannath and mahaprasad [both of] which have been placed before the god. (Gurung 1984, 123)

Gurung has observed the similarity to "modern techniques of sales promotion if we visualize Puri as a destination, Jatra as the best season, Pandas as hosts, batuwas as travel agents and nirmalya or mahaprasad as colourful brochures and discounted group rates!" He adds that "while the devout derive spiritual satisfaction from pilgrimage to a shrine (the farther the distance, the greater the sanctity), there is similarly an element of mental satisfaction and relaxation in modern travel for tourism" (Gurung 1984, 124).

But only in the nineteenth century did Americans and Europeans begin to tour purely for rest, relaxation, or education as, on the one hand, city dwellers sought in rural settings a respite from their work and, on the other, the socialization process of elites began to include the grand tour of Europe. Distant places, and the people in them, were idealized, and travel to such places seemed to offer an antidote to industrial civilization's discontent.[1] But modern mass tourism is an entirely new phenomenon, dating only from the mid-1960s, when industrial affluence, an expanding middle class, and relatively cheap commercial jet travel combined to make it possible.

Observers of tourism tend to divide into two camps (for more scholarly views see MacCannell 1976, Smith 1989, Graburn 1976). One camp's view, seconded by critics from the "tourist" side, is that the prize trophy caught in the tourist trap is the indigenous peoples who are its bait. On this account tourism ultimately dehumanizes and destroys the cultural integrity and richness of an area because it "places the whole of the visited culture on sale, distorting its imagery and symbolism, turning its emotions loose, transforming a way of life into an industry. . . . A culture . . . is turned from subject to object, from independent to dependent, from audience-in-its-own-right to spectacle" (Smith 1980, 60).

Khumbu tourists frequently fall into this camp, although their concern is typically with the degradation of the environment rather than of the culture, as is illustrated by the following comment entered in the visitor's log book of the national park lodge at Tengboche Monastery:

I fear the trend of "Industrial Tourism." Must we lead Nepal down the same [path to] ruination that so many of the Western nations have gone? They have paved with asphalt the area around "Old Faithful" geyser in Yellowstone National Park, Yosemite has smog and traffic jams, they have buried the beautiful Colorado River behind Glen Canyon Dam, and the Canadians have blasted the so-called Ice-fields Parkway right through their beautiful Jasper and Banff National Parks. Is that progress? Will the government's plan to build a road into this area improve it? or the lives of the people here? This spot, as well as the other beautiful and unique places on earth, should be considered the property of mankind, not a handful of developers, and should be treated with respect so that our children and their children can experience the beauty and solitude that we have all felt on this trek. If we want to help the people of Nepal, let's help them in real ways—better means of food production, schools, hospitals. Please, let's spare them from the garbage that is burying us.

Another trekker, sardonically inclined, expressed the same sentiments more tersely: "A hot shower, steaks, and 500-foot viewing tower with central heating would definitely be in order."

The opposite camp, more sanguine, views tourism as a boon because of the economic benefits it allegedly brings to indigenous peoples and their governments. Not surprisingly, central governments are generally persuaded by this argument, and His Majesty's Government of Nepal is no exception: earnings from tourism now form the backbone of the nonagricultural sector of the economy. But this development is very recent.

The Rana regime that ruled from 1846 to 1951 devoted most of its governmental energies to seeing that as little development (not to mention tourism) as possible took place. But even before it was overthrown, it had (like its predecessors) made some feeble and notably unsuccessful attempts to find exploitable mineral resources in the mountains. Even more energetic geological surveys since 1951 have not yielded much, however, and by the 1970s the Nepalese realized that their only substantial natural resource (other than hydroelectric power) was the art and architecture of the cities and the rugged scenery of the countryside that had been staring down at them all along. To enter the country to view these Nepalese treasures, foreign tourists would pay handsomely. Those who wanted to see and walk among the mountains would bring money to the often remote and poor rural villages. Only about 15 percent of all tourists to Nepal go trekking, but they account for 37 percent of the nights spent in Nepal (see Burger 1978); those going to Khumbu spend an average of twelve days there (see Bjonness 1979).

According to the fifth plan (1975–80; later plans are consistent with it), the development of tourism has three aims:

1. To earn foreign exchange and thus help to produce a balance of payments

2. To increase employment by developing local arts and handicrafts and to raise the purchasing power of the majority of people

3. To install tourist centers at appropriate places to promote regional balance and to encourage interregional and regional tourism

The first, and easiest, aim is being accomplished; according to the World Tourism Organization secretariat, international travel receipts for 1985 totaled $105 billion. The best way to assess whether the second and third aims are being accomplished is to examine the effects of tourism as they actually unfold in a particular mountain region. Khumbu is a best-case area for studying the local benefits of tourism: not only do large numbers of tourists visit the region (though they constitute less than a third of all trekkers to Nepal), but its inhabitants, unlike those who live in other trekking areas, also hold the most lucrative jobs in trekking, as sardars, cooks, sherpas, cook-boys, and—to a lesser but increasing extent—management jobs in the trekking companies in Kathmandu. The word *sherpa,* uncapitalized, has come to denote a job category—the sherpa assists the trekking party by setting up tents, managing loads, and doing whatever other tasks need to be done in the course of a trek.[2] Thus whatever local benefits of tourism exist should be most immediately and conspicuously evident in Khumbu, whose population is involved with tourism in the most, as well as the least, remunerative ways.

Any particular Sherpa may perform several or all of the trekking jobs at different times of his life. Typically, the first job, as porter or kitchen boy at about the age of fifteen, is followed after two or three years by the job of sherpa. Serious mountaineering could begin at about twenty, and by thirty one might be promoted to cook or sardar, depending on skills (command of English, leadership abilities, culinary talents, etc.).

METHODOLOGY

To explore the phenomenon of mountain tourism I returned to Khumjung-Khunde in the fall of 1978, collected basic demographic and economic data for all of Khumbu, and made a more detailed, comparative investigation of three villages and the monastery that serves them. Except where otherwise indicated, the data in this chapter describe conditions as they existed then.

For obvious geographical reasons Namche Bazaar is the Khumbu village most directly affected by tourism. Every tourist (every Sherpa, for that matter) who enters upper Khumbu from Nepal must first pass through Namche Bazaar, central gateway to the rest of Khumbu.[3] Given the long, tiring climb from the Dudh Koshi up to Namche, this village is also a natural stopping place for the night. Namche entrepreneurs have responded quickly to the economic opportunity tourists present by opening roughly twenty-five shops and hotels, which cater also to the three hundred or so Nepalese government officials who now live in Namche. More establishments are springing up all the time. By 1988

Fig. 64. In the International Foot Rest Hotel, now defunct, in Namche, trekkers rolled out their sleeping bags and spent the night for about twenty-five cents.

there were well over one hundred lodges and teashops above Lukla (Figs. 64–67).

The twin villages of Khumjung and Khunde are also strongly affected by tourism, but more indirectly. Located an hour's walk above Namche, they are slightly off the main trail to the major attractions of the area, such as Mt. Everest base camp. But large numbers of Khumjung and Khunde Sherpas work for trekking companies as sardars, cooks, sherpas, and cook-boys as well as ordinary porters.

The third village, Phortse, stands apart from the others as the most traditional, conservative village in all of Khumbu. It is also the village least affected by tourism.[4] Finally, the monastery nearest to these three villages is Tengboche. Most of its monks are drawn from these and nearby villages, and it is to Tengboche that villagers repair for Mani-Rimdu, the major religious rite of the year. It is also Tengboche's monks whom they call to officiate at funerals or to read the Tibetan texts that bring good fortune to a household.

Westerners—tourists and anthropologists alike—tend to think of Sherpa culture as essentially uniform, at least within Khumbu itself. But I found especially intriguing the differences among the three villages that were apparent in the extent to which they were involved in and

Fig. 65.   Meals can be ordered in such trekking lodges and in trailside tea-houses.

affected by tourism. In Khunde, 85 percent of all households had at least one person working in tourism as a sardar, cook, cook-boy, sherpa, or porter. In Phortse, by contrast, only 47 percent of the households had someone similarly employed. The relevant figures for all three villages are shown in Table 5. As the participation in tourism varies, so do the effects—not only quantitatively, but qualitatively.[5]

ECONOMIC IMPLICATIONS

As the village totals show, there are large sums of money to be earned in tourism, and the figures in Table 5 do not include the extras—tips, equipment, clothing that can be used or sold, and the like. The lion's share, 40 percent, of the tourist trekking dollar goes to the trekking

Fig. 66. Somewhat more upscale is the Sherpa Trekker's Lodge, built in 1979 with financing from the Nepal Industrial Development Corporation.

Fig. 67. Trekking facilities have sprouted in what were formerly summer *yersa* settlements; this lodge is in Dukla, at about 15,000 feet, on the way to the Everest base camp.

TABLE 5   EMPLOYMENT AND INCOME FROM TOURISM
IN SELECTED KHUMBU VILLAGES, 1978

Village	Households involved in tourism (percentage)	Individuals employed (total population in parentheses)	Yearly income (in Rs)	Mean earnings per individual (in Rs)
Namche	84	150 (540)	895,000	5,967
Khunde	85	68 (227)	304,100	4,472
Khumjung	76	113 (585)	479,280[a]	4,241
Phortse	47	35 (277)	184,850	5,281

[a]This figure does not include wages for portering water the mile or so from Khumjung to the Japanese-built luxury hotel Everest-View. From 1972 to 1982, about twenty families provided porters for this purpose, which cost the hotel as much as Rs 12,000 per month. The annual income of the Khumjung villagers who carried the water totaled roughly Rs 60,000. The hotel closed during the monsoon and had relatively few clients during the coldest months. In 1982, for lack of reliable air service to Syangboche, the hotel closed to all but local customers, but by 1988 it was being refurbished for another try.

companies themselves; the balance breaks down roughly as follows: trail expenses, 5 percent; food, 20 percent; Sherpas and other trail staff, 35 percent.

Of the twenty or so trekking companies registered in 1978, Sherpas had a majority financial interest in only four; by 1985 Sherpas owned about 30 percent of the companies. By 1988 there were about a hundred trekking and travel agencies in Kathmandu, most of them very small. Twenty-six of the fifty-six larger ones, those registered with the Nepal Trekking Agent Association, were controlled by Sherpas (Kunwar 1989). Five of the bigger trekking agencies employed a total of 94 permanent salaried staff, 70 employees during part of the year, and 670 at peak season.

The great majority of Khumbu Sherpas have never in their lives had access to such large amounts of cash. Much of this monetary gain, however, is consumed by inflation, exacerbated in Khumbu as ever-increasing numbers of tourists compete for the goods sold in the weekly bazaar in Namche (the competition would be more acute if half the food for organized groups were not bought in Kathmandu). Table 6, for the period 1964–85, gives some idea of the scale.

The table states in statistical form information Sherpas themselves are quick to volunteer: although they are earning unprecedented wages

TABLE 6   DAILY WAGES AND FOOD COSTS IN KHUMBU,
WITH PERCENTAGE INCREASES
(Base year 1964)

	1974	1978	1988	1964–88
Porter's wages	Rs 10 (67)	Rs 18 (80)	Rs 50 (180)	(730)
Sherpa's wages	Rs 15 (50)	Rs 25 (67)	Rs 65 (160)	(550)
Sardar's wages	Rs 25 (56)	Rs 35 (40)	Rs 75 (114)	(369)
Rice	Rs 26 (189)	Rs 35 (35)	Rs 90 (157)	(900)
Potatoes	Rs 14 (600)	Rs 20 (43)	Rs 25 (25)	(1,150)

Note: In 1964 wages and prices were as follows:
Porters   Rs 6 per day
Sherpas   Rs 10 per day
Sardars   Rs 16 per day
Rice   Rs 9 per pathi (4.36 liters)
Potatoes Rs 2 per tin

now, things are really much the same as they were before because the cost of living is even higher. But the purchasing power of the Sherpas has neither declined nor remained static since 1964 because in that year few Sherpas had tourist or mountaineering jobs. Since they are, in this sense, starting from scratch, their cash situation can only have improved.

To the extent that Sherpas grow most of the food they eat (unlike, for example, the Thakalis north of Pokhara), they are not affected by inflation. Indeed, since they grow their own potatoes and sell what they don't need, the astronomical inflation of this staple works to their benefit. But now Sherpas also buy as much rice, at its constantly inflating prices, as they can afford. This creates severe difficulties for the poorest families—those having little or no recourse to the financial benefits of tourism. The difficulties arise not because of the need to eat rice at home (there are always plenty of potatoes for domestic consumption) but because of the many social occasions on which it is culturally mandatory to serve expensive imported food. For example, whereas formerly buckwheat or potatoes were distributed at funerals or at the annual *Dumje* festival, now it would be humiliating to serve anything other than rice. Even the remuneration paid to lamas to read texts at private Sherpa houses has increased.

Sherpas whose cash is derived mainly from the sale of *dzom* or *zopkio* face great financial uncertainty since whether, and what, a yak will reproduce from year to year is highly uncertain. Whereas such animals are unreliable sources of income, herds of tourists have so far generated a dependable and even increasing annual income. Sherpas—those in the Thame Valley, for example—who have traditionally bartered the Tibetan tea they bring from Tibet face another type of difficulty. Khumjung Sherpas who work for tourists can now obtain Tibetan tea more cheaply by buying it in Kathmandu than by bartering for it with the Thame traders.

But the most dramatic economic change is the increase in employment. To obtain work with an expedition in 1964 or before, a Sherpa had to go to the sardar with a bottle of chang and ask for the privilege of carrying a load. By 1974 the situation was utterly reversed. I remember sardars for the Spanish Mt. Everest Expedition that year feverishly combing Khumbu villages for any spare animals or otherwise unemployable humans (like elderly women) who would carry their loads from Lukla to base camp. Another indication of the labor shortage is the disappearance of the chit books in which Sherpas carefully kept letters of reference written by expedition leaders for use in future job hunting. In a seller's market, such recommendations have become superfluous. Sherpas starting with little or no cash in 1964—certainly the vast majority—are in enviable economic positions today, and they know it.

But partly because of inflation, partly because the pay is seasonal, and partly because most Sherpas have little experience in modern business, they have saved and invested little. When asked what they have done with their substantial earnings, Sherpas reply, in Nepali, that they have "eaten" their money—and they usually mean that they now eat a more varied and expensive diet than previously. In Khumbu, this means not only more rice, once a luxury but now eaten as often as two or three times a week, but also more vegetables and fruits, some grown locally, the result of garden experiments by individual Sherpas.

The weekly bazaar in Namche, which did not even exist in 1964,[6] now offers a wide variety of fruits and vegetables. Before 1965 the village name Namche Bazaar was something of a misnomer, justified only by the stocks of goods, including rice, that many of its citizens, who were traders, kept in their houses. Although they transported most of the rice to Tibet on yaks, they would also sell locally on demand.

What Sherpas do not spend for other purposes (including religion) they spend primarily on jewelry or on repairing or upgrading their houses—by replacing traditional slate or wood roofs with sheets of corrugated iron, for example. In Kathmandu "eating" money can mean spending it not only on more expensive food but also on alcohol, parties, taxis, movies, and so on. Sherpas believe the Tibetan proverb they quote: "You don't become poor from eating, but from being lazy."

As there is much more to spend money on now, even within Khumbu (not only food, housing, and jewelry but also clothes and such modern items as watches and radios), incipient class differences are emerging as a new "tourist Sherpa" class begins to develop. This nouveau-riche group is distinguished by the novel source of wealth at its disposal (land and yak herds were the old bases of wealth) and the ostensibly different life-style it can buy. Formerly, too, there were great differences in wealth among families, but wealthy people looked and lived about the same as poor people—at least for most everyday, practical purposes. The wealthy did little with their money (other than host such feasts as *Dumje* more lavishly than poorer people could, or donate generously to religious projects, or wear more jewelry) that distinguished them from those who were less well-off. But with imported hiking boots, colorful wool sweaters, and down parkas, a trekking Sherpa is not hard to distinguish from a full-time, old-style potato farmer. New wealth is displayed; old wealth is camouflaged. In the absence of traditional wool garments, poorer Sherpas now have to pile on many layers of cotton to keep warm (see Fürer-Haimendorf 1975).

Another result of massive employment in tourism is that people no longer have time to do some of the things they did before. Time "has the great advantage that it is measurable and that it must be used in the satisfaction of any ends whatsoever" (C. S. Belshaw, quoted in Firth 1970, 20), and changing allocations of time clearly reflect changing livelihood patterns among Sherpas. Although increasingly precise measures of anything—including time—are possible, it is enough here to note that many Sherpas involved with tourism spend more time out of Khumbu than at home, and many Sherpas spend ten months a year away from their villages. There is certainly precedent for seasonal absences from home in the long-distance trading to Tibet, but the present trend has greatly increased both the number of Sherpas gone from Khumbu and the total time they are away.

Some traditional local crafts are dying out, not only because tourist jobs are more profitable but also because the supply of wood and wool is not as large or as dependable as it used to be. With so much cash on hand, people now tend to buy manufactured items; instead of making their own cloth, for example, they can easily buy Korean or Japanese cloth in the Namche shops. And instead of the traditional wooden

Fig. 68. Khumjung villagers line up to get water. Some of them will carry it a mile uphill to the Everest-View Hotel, which has no other source of water. The traditional heavy wooden water carrier, like the one at the head of the line, is being replaced by plastic jerry cans.

water carriers, which are heavy even when empty, people increasingly use lightweight plastic jerry cans (Fig. 68), part of the expeditionary flotsam and jetsam that have accumulated over the years.

Sales of Tibetan-style curios to tourists, however, are brisk. Salesmen—frequently Tibetan refugees—confront tourists as soon as they step off the plane at Syangboche or Lukla as well as at various places along the trails (Fig. 69), their wares spread out on a blanket or ground cloth. Almost all these curios are flown in from Kathmandu (and some of the items are made by Tibetans living in India), although tourists think they are getting the genuine article by coming to what they imagine is its true source. The only Tibetan curios that actually come from Tibet are yak bells, and even these are also made by blacksmiths (Kāmis) in Namche.

The job of school teacher, although certainly not an occupation with a long history in Khumbu, is another casualty of mass tourism (see chapter 3). Of thirty-three teachers spread over the five Khumbu schools, only two are Sherpas; the others are all non-Sherpa Nepalese. The same fate has befallen other skilled professions, such as carpenters

Fig. 69. A Tibetan lays out trinkets to sell to tourists who happen by on the trail.

and powerhouse operators for the new hydroelectric plant in Namche. Young Sherpas regard trekking jobs as much more attractive, although the advantages are somewhat illusory: teachers earn a regular monthly salary; most trekking jobs pay only during the actual trek and not between treks or during the off-season. Primary school teachers in Khumbu earn Rs 1,824 per month (including a 100 percent remote-area allowance); middle school teachers earn Rs 2,600 per month; and high school teachers earn Rs 3,300 per month (1979 figures). Sherpas, however, think not just of trekking jobs but of trekking careers, and the capstone to a career in trekking is the position of sardar. The hope of achieving this position draws the younger generation out of the schools and into tourism in large numbers.

A trekking sardar's income is highly variable, according to the policies and resources of the different trekking companies. But those who hold class A sardar positions (the highest of the three classes, A, B, and C) typically earn Rs 1,000 per month twelve months a year along with insurance and a pension, plus free food and an allowance of Rs 20 per day while trekking. Expedition sardars earn more. At Rs 50 per day, they would make Rs 1,500 per month, plus food and equipment. Or in lieu of equipment they might receive a lump sum payment (a recent trend) of anywhere from Rs 12,000 to Rs 25,000 for equipment for a two- or three-month expedition. High-altitude Sherpas are also eligible for bonuses, depending on how often they carry loads high on the mountain. By contrast, the chief warden at Sagarmatha National Park earns Rs 4,600 per month, with no allowance for food.

Lucrative as all this is, it represents only part of the sardar's income potential, for a trekking sardar can easily augment his income through graft since he acts as bursar for trekking groups on the trail. For example, if a sardar reports that he is employing thirty-five porters but actually has only thirty loads, he can pocket the wages of the five phantom porters—Rs 30 per day for each—for a daily profit of Rs 150 on top of his regular, legitimate, earnings. This is in addition to the practice common among sardars in Khumbu before the present labor shortage, and still practiced elsewhere in Nepal, of extracting a "commission" from porters in return for giving them jobs.

Even without illicit earnings, sardars can increase their income by using their own animals and relatives for portering, so that money is kept within the family. Less easily quantified is the help many Western clients give their favorite Sherpas. This ranges from the giving of *bakshis* (tips) at the end of a trek, to the donation of funds to send the Sherpas' children to school, to help with a medical problem, to the underwriting of a business venture, or to funding a visit to a foreign country. Moreover, various agencies and groups donate money and sponsor development projects in Solu-Khumbu: the Himalayan Trust, the American Himalayan Foundation, the Canadian Everest Society, Cultural Survival, and others. In 1989 Japanese interests donated Rs 50,000 for renovation of the Khumjung *gompa* in return for allowing the yeti scalp kept there to be displayed at an exposition in Nagoya.

There is an irony in the Sherpas' preference for trekking over teaching, since one of the main qualifications for Sherpas working with tourists nowadays is a knowledge of spoken and written Nepali and English, which they would not have if they had not attended one or the other of their local village schools. Thus they acquire literacy in schools, which they then abandon to take jobs that increasingly require an ability to read and write. In 1964 there was virtually no literacy in Nepali, not to mention English, among the Sherpas; by 1978, 157 Sherpas were literate in Nepali in Namche Bazaar; 174 in Khumjung; 57 in Khunde; and 51 in Phortse. Students in the upper classes tend to prefer the immediate rewards of trekking to the delayed gratification of further education. Even some of those attending college in Kathmandu play hooky during the trekking season to work for tourists. Some of the older mountaineering sardars recognize how fragile the trekking industry is—there is always the possibility of a decline either in the number of tourists or in the Sherpa share of the tourist dollar. These sardars want a university education for their children, but the children themselves generally want to get into trekking as soon as they can.

Another occupation that has suffered is agriculture. Beginning in the spring of 1974, Khumbu Sherpas began hiring Solu Sherpas in large numbers to work their fields while they themselves went off to pursue more lucrative trekking jobs. In 1978 a majority of the households in Khumjung-Khunde had at least one servant, paying them Rs 6 per day plus food for their labor while they themselves earned trekking wages and pocketed the difference (see Bjonness 1983). By 1988 the vast majority of load carriers in Khumbu were from Solu, as Khumbu Sherpas, typically keeping one step ahead, opened more lodges or worked in managerial, or "front-office," trekking jobs.

For a variety of reasons, including the tendency for hired labor to execute jobs less carefully than a landowner working his own land and the decrease in leaf litter that has accompanied deforestation, the general consensus is that there has been a slight drop in agricultural productivity. Sherpas are not alarmed by the decline, perhaps because it has been offset by the recent introduction of a strain of potato with three times the yield of the traditional variety. Sherpas prefer the taste of the old potato, however, and use the new variety to make pancakes, *rakshi*, and so on. They keep about 20 percent of their fields planted in the old strain, which they eat boiled.

Still, the feeling persists that crops are not what they used to be, and marginal, relatively unproductive fields—in high summer pastures, for example—are being abandoned for lack of workers to cultivate them. The strict rules designed to keep animals out of the village during the growing and harvest seasons are now very loosely enforced in Khumjung; by contrast, Phortse still observes these rules to the letter and still produces good crops—much better, it is commonly acknowledged by the inhabitants of both villages, than those in Khumjung.

Perhaps the greater danger of mass employment in tourism is that tourism itself is vulnerable to so many potential threats. A basic principle of ecological analysis, Liebig's law, states that an adaptation, to be viable over the long run, must be able to survive the most difficult conditions, as opposed to just the average conditions, that the environment imposes. Otherwise the strategic situation is similar to that of the nonswimming statistician who drowned trying to wade across a river whose average depth was only three feet.

Khumbu Sherpas have to worry about increased competition from Sherpas elsewhere in Nepal as well as from other groups, such as Tamangs. Already their monopoly even on mountaineering expeditions has been weakened. Of thirty-two high-altitude Sherpas employed by the American Mt. Everest Expedition in 1963, twenty-five were from Khumbu and only three from Solu (four were from Darjeeling). No large expedition today is likely to be staffed so overwhelmingly by Khumbu Sherpas. On the French Everest Expedition of 1988, for example, the twenty-eight Nepalese employed above base camp included one Gurung, one Tamang, and only seven Khumbu Sherpas (the remaining nineteen were non-Khumbu Sherpas). The notion that a Tamang or Newar could reach the summit of Mt. Everest (a Tamang made the ascent in 1973 and repeated it in 1985, when a Newar also reached the top) was not seriously entertained in 1963.

Sherpas must also face the possibility of such external threats as an economic recession, an oil embargo, political turmoil, or a government policy that discourages tourism. Because any of these factors could halt tourism overnight, its spectacular financial success is limited in the same way as the increased production of the green revolution, which depends on the availability of irrigation, fertilizer, and so on in the right amounts at the right times. Tourists in a remote place such as Khumbu are a new crop the Sherpas are raising on their steep mountain slopes, one as subject to environmental constraints, pressures, and disasters as any strain of miracle rice (Fig. 70). An even more appropriate analogy is the one Sherpas themselves use: tourists are like so many cattle, representing highly mobile, productive, and prestigious, but perishable, forms of wealth. Like cattle, tourists give good milk, but only if they are well fed.

IMAGES

TOURISTS

To understand tourism in Khumbu requires an understanding not only of Sherpas but also of their clients. Tourists want to come to Khumbu not only because they want to see Mt. Everest and the Himalayas but also because they like the Sherpas or like what they have heard or read about them either in a book about Sherpas specifically or in one about

Fig. 70. A Kathmandu trekking agency settles a large group of tourists in fields near Khumjung.

Nepal or mountaineering that mentions them. (Perhaps because of the sense of humor of tired trekkers who had hoped to escape from questionnaires in the Himalayas, the book tourists cited most frequently in our 1978 survey was *Tintin in Tibet*.) Having discovered that technology enables us to control nature without enhancing our experience of it or ourselves, we retreat to the high Himalayas to intensify our sense of both. Khumbu offers tourists the rare opportunity (rare because men and mountains meet so much more closely there than elsewhere in the Himalayas) to experience culture and nature, and their combination—high human adventure—at the top of the world (Figs. 71 and 72).

A kind of mutual admiration society exists between Sherpas and Westerners, and just why this should be so is an interesting question in itself. What is involved is the set of stereotyped images each group has of the other. Westerners have developed a positive image of Sherpas: that of an egalitarian, peaceful, hardy, honest, polite, industrious, hospitable, cheerful, independent, brave, heroic, compassionate people. This image begins on the basis of literary evidence, which has by now assumed epic proportions, and is reinforced, when everything goes well, by personal experience in the course of a trek.

This image reflects not only what Westerners think about Sherpas but also what Sherpa culture itself values in human beings. So far as it goes, the image captures one side of the Sherpa personality—but only one side. Like all people, Sherpas wear masks (see p. 1). They have a public, onstage, side that they want the rest of the world to see and a private, backstage, side that is more unadornedly true to themselves. Although the qualities that characterize the public side are also present—and are in fact rooted—in the private side, so are other, less praiseworthy, types of behavior.

One of the difficulties for Sherpas working on a tourist trek—a twenty-four-hour-a-day job—is maintaining the onstage image full-time, a task that would vex a saint. Successful trekking Sherpas realize that they are, in part, paid professional actors and entertainers. Their stories and dances and songs are genuine enough, but they are also what clients want. And what clients pay for, they get. Only when the trek is over and the backstage self can be safely unveiled at home do the Sherpas engage in drinking binges and general hell-raising that may go on for days.

In addition to alcoholism there are other less salutary sides to Sherpa character. For example, because of their international mobility Sherpas can easily smuggle contraband such as gold and drugs. This activity can provide money to support life-styles of ever-escalating luxury, comfort, and ease. It can also land the Sherpas in foreign jails. But none of this backstage behavior is included in the official image.

The original, pre-Lukla airstrip (1964), image Sherpas held of Westerners was one of technologically sophisticated, generous, wealthy, irrationally adventurous, egalitarian, and well-intentioned, if not always physically strong, people. This more or less coherent image was formed on the basis of contact with a small number of relatively homogeneous people, mostly mountaineers and the occasional hardy trekker. But in recent years this image has given way to a less clearly focused one that has emerged out of the Sherpas' experiences with thousands upon thousands of tourists—everyone from the psychotic French woman who had to be straitjacketed and evacuated to the American who has taken the vows of a lama to the German divorcée in search of romance. Although the original positive image still holds, foreigners are now equally likely to be thought crude, stumbling, demanding, arrogant, unpredictable, and cheap. Where foreigners are concerned, Sherpas have learned to have no stable expectations. So much for unitary images.

Westerners are enchanted with Sherpas because the qualities the

Figs. 71 and 72.   Not all tourists are adults, as these pictures of my children, Kim (*above*) and Maya (*opposite*), show. Ang Urkien, daughter of the late Sardar Changchu, who spent the year 1968–69 in Dolpa with me, carries Maya.

Sherpas are thought to possess are not only those Westerners admire but also precisely those they feel they should embody but conspicuously lack or do not adequately measure up to. So Sherpa society, or the Western image of it, represents a dramatic realization of what Westerners would like to be themselves, hence their frequently breathless enthusiasm for the Sherpas.

There is also probably a measure of admiration for what Westerners regard as the liberal Sherpa sexual ethic, and in this there are precedents (both in the anthropological reporting and in the public reaction to it)

in earlier work by Margaret Mead and B. Malinowski among the is-
landers of the South Pacific.

Although the causes, strength, and justification of the mutual admiration may be debated, there is clearly an affinity between Westerners
and Sherpas, as evidenced by the high rate of intermarriage (Fig. 73).
There have been forty or so cases of marriage between Westerners
and Sherpas, almost all relatively uneducated villagers from Solu or
Khumbu (Fürer-Haimendorf 1985). And there have been many more
informal liaisons, primarily between trekking sardars and their Western
female clientele. (Similar liaisons occurred in the Alps in the nineteenth
century.) These liaisons reverse the more typical tourist situation elsewhere in the world, where single tourists are apt to be males traveling
in pursuit of interests both exotic and erotic.

MOUNTAINS AND MOUNTAINEERING

Although it is the environment of Khumbu that attracts Western tourists, their perception of that environment, ironically, is fundamentally
incompatible with that of the Sherpas. The most general Sherpa term
for beautiful (*lemu*) can apply to the physical features as well as the
personal qualities of human beings, both men and women. It can also
apply to inanimate objects and to the environment as a whole. But

Fig. 73. Sherpas marry not only foreigners but also non-Sherpa Nepalese, a practice for which there is ample historical precedent. This young Tamang woman, Phul Maya, married Nima Norbu of Namche; in the mid-1970s, when this photograph was taken, they had five children, including two sets of twins.

while a field or forest might be *lemu,* the giant snow peaks towering in every direction over Khumbu are never considered *lemu.* Their lack of color (their whiteness) is seen as uninteresting (though religiously significant)—not a surprising judgment in view of the Sherpa preference for vivid colors evident in such disparate contexts as religious paintings and women's aprons. A snow peak elsewhere might be admired for its shape, and Pertemba (see Fig. 61), one of the foremost Sherpa sardars of his time, says that one of the pleasures he derives from climbing is the beauty of the different views from high on a mountain. But generally familiarity has bred indifference rather than awe, and the shape of the Khumbu snow and ice peaks is just too boring to be considered *lemu.*[7] Even the dramatic setting of Tengboche Monastery is said to have been selected without regard to its beauty. It was chosen by name, sight unseen, because the footprints of Lama Sangwa Dorje, a seminal figure in Sherpa history who was born about 350 years ago, had been embedded in rock when he stopped there.[8]

Sherpas pay close attention to their environment nonetheless, and not just to those features of it that are economically important. They often find familiar shapes in mountains or villages, much as Westerners find them in clouds. To Sherpas, Phortse looks either like a *damar,* a rattle lamas use during rituals, or like an animal hide stretched out to dry. And together the villages of Khumjung and Khunde resemble a horse whose rider is Khumbi Yul Lha, the peak that rises above them (see Fig. 1).

Sherpas are generally mystified that Westerners come to Khumbu at such great expense and in such great numbers, whether to trek or to climb. Even the most experienced sardars admit they cannot fathom why Europeans climb, though they make guesses. One hunch is that they climb for fame, since the books they write always include plenty of pictures of themselves. But Sherpas also know that books are bought, so a second hypothesis is that people climb to make money. One sardar, for example, thought this was the case with the British mountaineer Chris Bonnington since he has written (and presumably sold) so many books; but the same sardar believed that fame drives Reinhold Messner (the first climber to ascend all fourteen 8,000-meter peaks) to the summits. Another sardar wondered whether science was not the prime motivation, while still another held that climbers climb to clear their minds from the worries of office work. If he were an office worker, he said, he might well need to clear his mind too, but if so he would do it by going on a weekend picnic rather than by climbing.

Eight of Khumbu's most experienced and illustrious sardars unanimously agreed that virtually the only reason they climb is that they need the high income they cannot earn any other way. As one put it, if he had the education to qualify for a good office job, he would unhesitatingly choose that line of work. Sherpas see no intrinsic point in climbing: neither fame (though that is welcome since it helps them get their next climbing job more easily; it also accounts for the multiple ascents of Everest), nor challenge, nor adventure. Climbing is simply a high-paying job. None of the eight sardars expressed much enthusiasm for a hypothetical all-Sherpa expedition because they could not imagine any earnings accruing from it. Even though they enjoy the camaraderie and the scenic views and take pride in a job well done, these reasons alone would never motivate them to move up a mountain. Plans for a "First Sherpa Youth Mt. Everest Expedition '91" indicate contrary sentiments, but if skilled Sherpa climbers are paid on such an expedition, the view of the eight sardars will stand unchallenged.

Women are left behind during a climb with the difficult task of managing the household, but those affected see the inconvenience as a relatively minor one, for which they are compensated by the pay earned. Sherpas see danger as by far the most negative feature of climbing. Their friends' deaths, one after the other over the years, make them vividly aware of the risks. Their wives and parents, although they welcome the earnings, universally oppose expedition work because of the danger. But the climbing Sherpas' view is that danger comes with the territory; they just hope they can learn enough from the deaths of their friends to avoid their mistakes. They judge that climbing is a hard but good job in which the benefits balance the risks—a view probably shared by Nepal's other big foreign exchange earners, the Gurkha soldiers who are paid to fight and die for Britain and India. Climbing Sherpas compare deaths on a mountain favorably with those of soldiers and taxi drivers, whose lives, unlike their own, are not insured. Those who feel that the difference in pay and the perks do not justify the greater risks of climbing choose trekking, although many do both, depending on the vagaries of opportunity and their own fluctuating financial needs.

Sardar Pertemba, like many climbing/trekking Sherpas, abandoned his studies and started working earlier than he might have because of the English he had learned at his village school (he also points out that knowing English will not get you to the top of the mountain). Although Pertemba likes both climbing and trekking, the work he enjoys most is the teaching he has done at the government mountaineering school in Manang. Most Sherpas learn to climb not from foreign mountaineers but from other Sherpas, usually between base camp and camp 1 on their first expedition. Pertemba thinks Sherpas need a mountaineering school in Khumbu to train young Sherpas properly and systematically in mountaineering techniques. Such a school would also generate income locally for experienced climbing Sherpas.

Although Sherpas do not consider mountains aesthetic monuments, they are not indifferent to all peaks. Some, like Khumbi Yul Lha, rising behind Khumjung-Khunde, are sacred by virtue of the deities that reside on them. Sherpas were reluctant to climb Karyolang, because of its sacredness, during the first all-Nepal expedition to that peak in 1975. They had no such compunctions about Kwangde, the second objective of the expedition, and proceeded to the top, as it turned out, of the east peak, which they mistook for the summit. Whether for spiritual reasons Sherpas would have been reluctant to attempt the summits of Khumbu in 1907, when they first began climbing in Sikkim, is an interesting but unanswerable historical question. Certainly no such general reluctance exists today. Not only the mountains but also some of their spirituality may have eroded over the years.

Khumbu must now be one of the most thoroughly mapped regions on the face of the earth, with vernacular names for virtually all prominent features of the landscape, but this detailed nomenclature is often a creation of foreign cartographers.[9] When I visited Everest base camp in 1964, Kala Pathar (black ridge), now one of the most popular trekking destinations in Nepal, was unnamed.

All this increasing specificity of geographical detail is evidence of the reversal of values that historically made Solu, with its lower elevation, more fertile fields, and more salubrious climate, the more highly valued land. According to one account, the earliest Sherpa pioneers settled first in the more hospitable climate of Solu, and the latecomers or impoverished Solu Sherpas had to settle for the harsher, more rugged landscape of Khumbu. Now, however, Khumbu is the center of prosperity, thus demonstrating that a resource acquires worth only when technology, values, and a market for it simultaneously converge.

SOCIAL

Sherpa and Western concepts of pollution constitute yet another example of cultural incompatibility. The Sherpa concept of pollution, called *tip* (see Ortner 1973), has nothing to do with the environmental effects of discarded tin cans, plastic, and rubber that concern so many Westerners—porters and Sherpas are responsible for the bulk of non–toilet paper litter (Figs. 74–78). Sherpas do not care one way or the other about this Western-style pollution because their concept of pollution concerns only the self, or human creations and artifacts, such as houses. *Tip* is a feeling, a moral state of mind, and is not generated ultimately from empirical observation of the natural world. For example, pollution can have religious causes, such as an imbalanced relationship with deities or contact with supernatural beings. Or it can be induced socially by contact with certain kinds of people, such as low-caste Nepali blacksmiths (Kāmis), of whom there are a few families in Namche and one in Khumjung, or members of the Tibetan butcher

Fig. 74. In the early morning, Sherpas burn juniper branches to purify themselves of *tip*. The cumulative effect of such purifying fires in Khumjung is that
smoke fills the morning air.

class, another low-ranked group. Westerners would surely, if they were
aware of these discriminations, moderate their views of egalitarian
Sherpa society. They would be even more likely to modify their views if
they realized that they themselves are a source of *tip* and that at least
until very recently Thame Sherpas returning from an expedition had to
be purified before they were allowed back in their houses. But since all
Westerners must come to the Sherpas via the far more obviously hierarchical Hindu societies to the south, they are lulled into ascribing an
egalitarian ideology to the Sherpas that simplifies, if it does not down-
right distort, the ethnographic facts.

But I do not want to leave the impression that Sherpas and their
clients pass like ships in the night, completely misperceiving one another. The Sherpa-trekker relationship is, as these things go in the world
of tourism, an unusually long and intensive one. Even though, as in any
person-to-person interaction, only behaviors relevant to the encounter
are exhibited—we never play all our roles at the same time—nevertheless Sherpas and their clients get to know one another over an extended
period of time, rarely less than a week, often a month or more.

Exigencies of living break down what might otherwise be a formal,
distant relationship: the Sherpas are in their element, perfectly accli-

matized, doing well what they have always done naturally—walking, carrying loads, enduring cold weather. The Westerners, by contrast, are usually out of shape, tired, plagued by sore muscles and blisters, and gasping for air. Sherpas are paid to be helpful under these conditions, and they are. They are even heroic, as the many stories of Sherpas who have died trying to rescue their clients on high peaks attest. And they are cheerful, hardworking, and eager to please, so in the end a relationship of trust and respect is built that would be impossible with a guide on a half-day tour of Kathmandu.

WESTERNIZATION

Are Sherpas being Westernized? By many visible indexes they are (Fig. 79). First, they wear Western-style clothing—pants, shirts, down jackets, and climbing or hiking boots. (Women's clothes have not changed from the indigenous Tibetan style, thus conforming to the female sartorial conservatism that has generally been the rule all over South Asia.) It is significant, however, that Khumbu Sherpas wear either Sherpa clothes (even the best-equipped mountaineering Sherpa wears the traditional Tibetan coat on ceremonial occasions [Fig. 80]) or Western dress but never the Nepali national dress. When His Majesty King Birendra visited the government yak farm at Syangboche in 1974, the *pradhan panchas* of both the Khumjung and Namche panchayats greeted him with sport coats and neckties, not *daura-suruwal,* the national dress. (At a formal reception in Kathmandu for members of the Nepal-China-Japan Everest Expedition in 1988, attended by the king, however, Sherpas did wear *daura-suruwal.*)

Similarly, although Sherpas recognize the importance and desirability of mastering the national language in both its spoken and written forms (Fig. 81), a Sherpa who uses too much Nepali in an otherwise purely Sherpa conversation in Khumbu is felt to be putting on airs.

Through association with trekkers as well as extensive travel abroad in the lands from which the trekkers come, Sherpas have gained a wide knowledge of modern hygiene, Western languages (including Japanese), and material culture generally. The tradition of drinking Tibetan salt-and-butter tea has largely disappeared in Sherpa homes (because of the high price of butter and the uncertain supply of Tibetan tea). Western ways are admired because Western contacts have opened new channels of mobility and access to power, wealth, and prestige. Sherpas honor the West because their experience of it has been so overwhelmingly positive financially.

Figs. 75, 76, 77, and 78.   Attempts to deal with garbage include a sign made by a Namche group (*top of page*), a Nepali sign saying Let's keep villages clean, and a rubbish pit dug by the national park (*opposite, top of page*). Traditional Sherpa material culture (*opposite*) is biodegradable. Much of what tourists bring with them is not.

Fig. 79. A Sherpa from the Chaurikharka area who flew into Lukla from Kathmandu stops on his way up the Dudh Koshi valley in his three-piece suit, attaché case in hand.

My own view is that such matters as clothing styles and diet are relatively superficial; much more important is the Sherpas' success in maintaining a cultural identity that is strongly and exclusively Sherpa. Sherpas tend not to be self-depreciating; whatever they are, they are mostly proud of it. Even those Sherpas who have achieved the greatest success, through mountaineering accomplishments or university educations, think of themselves primarily and uncompromisingly as Sherpas.

Part of the reason for this tenacious cultural identity is the mutual admiration of Westerners and Sherpas that I have already mentioned.

Fig. 80. Ang Rita, my assistant, wears a traditional formal Sherpa coat (*chuwa*) en route to a marriage ceremony (*dem-chang*) for his brother.

Sherpas are so massively reinforced at every point for being Sherpas that they have every reason not only to "stay" Sherpa but even to flaunt their Sherpahood. One might say that tourists pay Sherpas in part for being Sherpa, or at least for performing the role that accords with the popular image of Sherpas. Nor are the advantages of the Sherpas' status lost on other groups in Nepal. Tamangs, for example, frequently try to pass themselves off as Sherpas. This process of "Sherpaization" counters the momentum of the much-vaunted Sanskritization (emulation of high Hindu caste behavior) that has absorbed the upward-mobilizing energies of the subcontinent for centuries.

As evidence of the reinforcement Sherpas have received for their pride and independence, a number of the more successful among them in recent years have dropped the suffix saheb and address their Western clients by their first names—something no house servant, hotel servant, or tour guide in Kathmandu would dream of doing. Westerners often react favorably to being treated as equals, even by someone waiting on them hand and foot. But some of them, accustomed to or expecting more traditional hierarchical relations between servant and master, are taken aback by the I'm-just-as-good-as-you Sherpa personality.

Because the "tourist Sherpas" still identify themselves very much as

Fig. 81. Despite occasional friction between Sherpas and government personnel, His Majesty's Government has made attempts to communicate with Sherpas, by printing the national anthem in Tibetan, for example.

Sherpas, no class of marginal people—neither fully Sherpa nor Western—has developed, as it often does in such contact situations. (The sexual differentiation that exists between Sherpa men and women is being maintained by differential access to education and jobs: there are occasional Sherpani [Sherpa women] "cook-boys" but only one Sherpani sardar so far.) The "tourist Sherpa" is not marginal to his society at all but fully accepted within its fold. Even Sherpas who live ten months of the year in Kathmandu keep their houses and fields and often their families in Khumbu. One Sherpa who has lived in Kathmandu for more than fifteen years, ten months of the year, now holds a high and trusted position (as *chorumba*) in the civil-religious hierarchy in his village. He is able to return to his village during the *Dumje* festival, in early summer, when his presence is essential. Even though he is hardly ever in his village, his status there does not diminish. On the contrary, his success in the travel business in Kathmandu has endorsed and enhanced it.

INTENSIFICATION

Rather than becoming Westernized or nationalized, then, Sherpa culture has been intensified. That is, Sherpas have come to value some of their traditions even more than they did prior to the advent of tourism. For example, although nowadays Sherpas rarely commission the carving of prayers on stones to be placed on the prayer walls at the entrance of villages (see Fig. 95), there seems to be no lessening of faith in Buddhist doctrine, and interest and participation in the many Buddhist rituals are as strong as ever. Some Sherpas claim that interest in religion has deepened, and some of the most successful and "Westernized" Sherpas are among the most devout.

Certainly the most educated Sherpas are still committed Buddhists who believe in and rely on their lamas' liturgical and ecclesiastical powers. In 1981 the Tengboche rimpoche was able to raise $20,000 in two days for a new *gompa* in Kathmandu. Kalden Sherpa (see pp. 69 and 94), owner of a flourishing trekking company, considered himself a Christian in 1963 (Hillary 1964) after two years in a Catholic boarding school, but he is now one of the most generous supporters of Tengboche Monastery; he personally financed the higher studies of four *thawas* at this Kathmandu *gompa*.

Sherpas not only have maintained their cultural identity and intensified it but also have contributed to making generally Tibetan lifestyles respectable in Nepal among Hindu and Hinduized Nepalese. In the first place, the status of hero is accorded anyone who has climbed Mt. Everest—recognition in the press, praise by the prime minister, and an audience with the king, thus turning the job of high-altitude porter into a distinguished and honorable occupation. Those so honored through 1988 include forty Nepalese Sherpas (some with multiple ascents, including two who have climbed the peak five times—one without ever using oxygen—two who have climbed it three times, and four who have climbed it twice), one Tamang (who has climbed it twice), one Newar, and several Darjeeling Sherpas. (By the end of 1988 there had been 261 ascents of Mt. Everest by a total of 228 men and 9 women.)

Sherpa success at high altitudes coincided with a surge of interest in things Tibetan after the great publicity given the Dalai Lama's retreat from Lhasa in 1959. Then after the 1962 China-India border war, when India placed severe restrictions on travel by foreigners into the Indian Himalayas and closed such traditional centers of Tibetan culture as Kalimpong to Westerners, Kathmandu became a place not only for foreigners to experience the culture of Tibetan refugees but for Bhutanese, Sikkimese, and Tibetan nobility and entrepreneurs (and, increasingly as time went on, rich Tibetan refugees) to live and work. Being wealthier than most Nepalese, they frequented the more elegant hotels and restaurants in their traditional dress. Thus their costume ceased to be identified only with the lowly Bhotias and became accepted as the standard apparel of wealthy, sophisticated, powerful people.

As all these developments combined to raise the status of Sherpas in the eyes of their countrymen, the female dress of Sherpas or Tibetans changed from an object of scorn, from the Hindu point of view, to high fashion—worn in the fashionable restaurants, hotels, and discotheques of Kathmandu, and on board Royal Nepal Airlines Corporation aircraft on international and domestic flights by women who would not have dreamed of wearing anything but a sari a few years before. A telling case in point is that of a Namche Sherpani who married a wealthy Newar and moved to Kathmandu in the late 1950s (see the photographs on the title page). During her first few years in Kathmandu she wore a sari, trying to blend in with her husband's milieu. By the 1970s she had reverted to her Sherpa dress, although this time with a more modish, tailored cut. By the 1980s her tastes had become eclectic—sometimes she wore a Sherpa dress, sometimes a sari, sometimes slacks, blue jeans, or a Western dress.

POLITICAL IMPLICATIONS

Although Sherpa culture is being intensified rather than adulterated, tourism is nevertheless accelerating the last stage of nation building in what would otherwise still be a remote and inaccessible area. Until 1964, when then Crown Prince Birendra made one of the first landings at Lukla to dedicate the new school at Chaurikharka (see Fig. 35), no high-level government official had ever visited Khumbu. Now His Majesty as well as such high officials as the zonal commissioner has visited Khumbu many times (Fig. 82). In 1964 the government's presence in Khumbu was represented by a post office and police checkpost in

Fig. 82. King Birendra (*leading, in uniform*) inspects a government yak farm.

Namche.[10] By 1978 two airstrips had been added along with a mete-
orological station, a government yak farm, village panchayat secre-
taries from outside Khumbu, a medical center, a bank providing such
services as savings accounts and cashing of travelers' checks, a police
checkpost in Thame, and a national park that includes all of Khumbu
(excluding, technically, the villages themselves).

Sherpas have viewed most of these institutions as either helpful or
harmless. But initially, at least, the primary feeling about Sagarmatha
National Park (Sagarmatha is the Nepali word for Everest) has been
one of fear. The main impact of the park so far has been to enforce
strictly the law against cutting green wood for fuel, and since no realistic alternative has been provided, Sherpa concern is understandable.
Much of the fear is based on rumors about even worse regulations still
to come, such as one that would prohibit Sherpas from gathering leaf
litter in the forests.

Sagarmatha National Park is in the unenviably ambiguous position
of having no authority to control or advise on large development projects sponsored by other agencies (such as the Austrian-aided hydroelectric project near Thame) even though as the paramount political
authority it has had an enervating effect on once-strong local institutions.[11]

The traditional forest wardens (*shing nawas*) had ceased functioning by the early 1970s (although they were still active in Phortse) as the astronomical sums tourists paid for firewood had led to massive cutting that systematically undermined the forest wardens' authority (Fig. 83). In 1982 honorary forest wardens were appointed from each panchayat ward, but they have not had much effect because they were given no authority to levy fines. All this is in dramatic contrast to 1964, when firewood was free for the asking to any overnight visitor in Solu-Khumbu.

The consumption of wood is strongly influenced not only by numbers of tourists but also by their trekking style (Figs. 84 and 85). Seventy percent of Khumbu trekkers in 1978 belonged to organized groups, which carry their own tents and food, while 30 percent stayed in local lodges—teahouse trekkers, as they are known in the trade (Bjonness 1979). The big groups use more wood because they are big (there are two or three porters or Sherpas for each tourist) and because their Sherpas make their own, usually inefficient, cooking fires and keep their clients cozy with bonfires. Teahouse trekkers, on the other hand, require fewer support personnel and keep warm in the lodges. As year-round lodges have sprung up almost all the way to Everest base camp, Khumbu trekkers are increasingly likely to be the individuals and small groups who patronize them. Kerosene is so prohibitively expensive compared with firewood that only hotels and lodges can afford to use it. Moreover, national park officials can monitor fuel use and enforce regulations much more readily in fixed sites than they can among nomadic trekking groups.

Sherpas say that the national park is now their forest warden. The traditional rule that enjoined Sherpas from cutting green trees applied only to forests near the villages, and the fine for breaking it (a bottle of beer) was mild. National park officials attempt to enforce the rule everywhere, far from the villages as well as near them, and punishment for infractions includes heavy fines and imprisonment.

Sagarmatha National Park has an impact even in areas where it does not belong. When the national park dedicated a new trekkers' lodge on the grounds of Tengboche Monastery, a chicken was sacrificed—not as part of the dedication ceremonies but by some Nepalese officials on their own. Officially or unofficially, the sacrifice of an animal near a monastery, of all places, was resented by the lamas, who refuse to kill even insects.

The deterioration of local political institutions cannot be explained

Fig. 83.   One of the repercussions of tourism is the destruction of live trees to provide fuel for cooking and campfires. A kerosene depot at the entrance to Sagarmatha National Park is part of an effort to stem this destruction. The national park has also established tree nurseries as part of an attempt at reforestation.

by the existence of the national park alone. Even if the local village panchayats did not feel preempted by the park, tourist jobs have lured away virtually everyone with leadership abilities. To serve effectively in the panchayat it is generally necessary to reside in the area. But as one influential local leader put it, anybody with any ambition, brains, or ability is off working for tourists most of the time, so there are too few competent people left to serve on the panchayats. The result is that panchayat members are either capable leaders who are often absent

Figs. 84 and 85.   The trail to the top of the Tengboche ridge in 1950 (*above*) and 1988 (*opposite*). Contrary to the alarmist view that the forests are rapidly disappearing, those on this hillside seem to have held their own and perhaps have even spread. The ground cover beneath the trees, however, may have been overgrazed. The earlier photograph is by Charles Houston.

from Khumbu, residents with little interest in politics, or, in one case, the wife of a local leader who serves as a surrogate for her politically important but frequently absent husband.

Both factors—the supremacy of the national park and the lack of leaders who stay put in Khumbu long enough to take an active part in political affairs there—have led to a fragmentation of village interests, with different individuals or groups promoting separate aims: the Everest-View Hotel, the trekking companies, the Himalayan Trust, the

panchayats, the national park, and so on. Whatever forces united a village politically in the past seem to have weakened in the face of all the external interests that now assert themselves. This fragmentation of interests is reflected in the lack of consensus on the importance of keeping animals out of the fields of Khumjung, described earlier.

DEMOGRAPHIC CONSEQUENCES

The major demographic consequence of tourism is the large outflow of young men from Khumbu for the better part of the year. There are two reasons for this emigration: one is to avoid the inflated social obligations that bankrupt those not involved in tourism (the "social budget" is now estimated to exceed the "domestic budget," though less in villages like Phortse or Thame than in Khumjung-Khunde). The other is to earn the money trekking jobs bring in.

One consequence of the long seasonal absences among the Sherpas is a lower birth rate and a concentration of births nine months after the summer monsoon season.[12] Other demographic consequences of tourism and mountaineering include high mortality rates for young men: from 1950 through the middle of 1989, eighty-four Sherpas died on mountaineering expeditions in Nepal (this figure excludes the many Sherpas killed on Everest, K2, and elsewhere between the world wars).[13] The great majority of these were Khumbu Sherpas, and the mortality rate among adult males is therefore quite high. But the existence of polyandry (although younger Sherpas now scorn the custom) and the easy remarriage of widows diminish the effects such deaths might have on the birth rate.

A much greater difference in the birth rate has been effected by the family-planning techniques made available through the Khunde Hospital. Contraception has re-created the relatively low fertility conditions that polyandry had produced before; the former results in fewer children per family, the latter in fewer families. Sherpas simultaneously love children and view them as difficult and demanding to raise, an attitude that provides a traditional basis for an interest in family planning.

The practice of family-planning measures seems to be influenced by the degree of participation in tourism. In Khunde, with only seven exceptions, all fertile women who had living husbands and two or more living children were practicing some form of birth control. Of these, fourteen had accepted IUDs, and three were taking pills. By contrast, in Phortse not a single woman had accepted a loop, three had received long-lasting injections (Depo-Provera), seven had tried pills but six of these had stopped taking them (some of whom had since become pregnant), and nineteen were not practicing any form of contraception. The fact that only seven women were not practicing contraception in Khunde, compared with nineteen in Phortse (two villages of about the same size) can be explained by the degree to which the inhabitants of each village have been drawn into the modern world through tourism and mountaineering. The economic importance of children declines quickly in an economy based on tourism rather than agriculture or transhumant nomadism.

The Sherpa medical assistant at Khunde Hospital reports that

Phortse women are too shy to ask for loops and are reluctant to ask for any other form of contraception, whereas for Khunde women such devices are accepted as an everyday fact of life. It is true that the hospital is located in Khunde and not in Phortse, but more than mere physical proximity is involved, since for any Phortse woman it is only a two-hour walk to Khunde—no great distance by Khumbu standards. Many Phortse women come within a few minutes of Khunde on their trips to the weekly bazaar at Namche on Saturdays, when the clinic is closed.

A final demographic consequence is the dispersal of the population to previously unoccupied areas of Khumbu or to sites once occupied only seasonally and now inhabited permanently. One example is the Syangboche area, site of the airstrip that serves the Everest-View Hotel. Only one family has moved here on a permanent basis (a recently prospering Kāmi family from Namche), but many other Sherpas stay in Syangboche for longer periods of time at the hotels, lodges, and tea shops that have sprung up there. If a piped-water system is ever devised to supply water to Syangboche (water at present must be carried from Khumjung-Khunde or from a seasonal spring above Namche), the Syangboche settlement will no doubt grow considerably.

With the opening of teahouses and hotels by entrepreneurs in such places as Phungi Tenga (at the bottom of the hill leading to Tengboche), Pheriche, Dingboche, Lobuche, and Gorak Shep—all formerly inhabited only in the summer months but now occupied the year round—the population has further dispersed. A different example of the same phenomenon is the concentration of Sherpas in an area of Kathmandu, Jyatha Tole, now known only half-jokingly as Sherpa Tole. By the late 1980s the more financially successful Sherpas were moving out of the cramped and congested bazaars of the capital to its airier and more fashionable suburbs.

CONCLUSION

The immediate future promises more of the same. If one or another of the dire events mentioned earlier, such as an oil embargo, were to transpire, most Sherpas would be able to return to their traditional means of livelihood; they even state that they would be happy to do so. Whether they really would be happy cannot be known before the event, but the more important point is that they have not burned their economic or psychological bridges behind them. Those who have been suf-

Fig. 86. The Tengboche rimpoche in 1950 at age fifteen, just after his period of study in monasteries in Tibet. Photograph by Elizabeth Cowles, from H. W. Tilman, *Nepal Himalaya*.

ficiently educated would have the option of obtaining office jobs in Kathmandu and elsewhere.

According to the law of evolutionary potential, the more general an adaptation of an organism or population to its environment, the greater its potential to evolve into something else; the more specialized the adaptation, the fewer the options available for further growth. Such specialized adaptations are inherently fragile, but Sherpas are fortunate in that their economic options remain open. Unlike inhabitants of other parts of the world heavily involved in tourism, most Sherpas will be able, if necessary, to return to their traditional ecological niche, even if the hotel and shop owners of Namche will have several useless buildings and facilities on their hands.

There is little scope for the further growth of tourism in Khumbu now, primarily because Royal Nepal Airlines Corporation is severely limited in the number of tourists it can fly to Lukla. The completion of the Lamosangu-Jiri road has probably brought a few more trekkers, but it has not broken the transportation bottleneck. The number of tourists as of the late 1970s was just under 4,000, up from 20 in 1964. In 1985 the number had reached about 5,000, and by 1986, it had

Fig. 87. The rimpoche in 1964 in his private study (note the Sears Formica and aluminum table with the biscuit tin, traditional Tibetan tea cups, and the customary donations from his guests).

climbed to 6,909.[14] In Namche, hotels keep springing up to accommodate the increasing numbers of teahouse trekkers, even though the number of tourists remains the same. If lodges are overbuilt, profits will be split into an increasing number of shares, or some businesses will prosper at the expense of others.

I have argued above that religious belief remains intact, but the population of the monastery at Tengboche has not. By 1978 there were so few monks that the Tengboche rimpoche (Figs. 86–88) had to import four from Thame just to have enough personnel to perform Mani-Rimdu, the biggest monastery celebration of the year. By 1985 the pendulum had begun to swing the other way. Substantial contributions from foreigners and increased receipts from tourist lodges owned by the monastery (in such places as Namche and Lobuche) resulted in improved living facilities, which made the monastic life feasible for more monks than it had been when each monk had to be self-supporting.

No carved stones for the *mani* walls have been commissioned for years,[15] and Sherpas say there are fewer readings of sacred texts (a day's reading still costs nine *manas* of rice, but nine *manas* cost much more now than formerly). Some Sherpas think religion as a belief system is

Fig. 88. The rimpoche in 1988, when he oversaw the construction of a new dormitory for monks. Some admired his progressive, activist spirit and interest in development projects; others criticized him for straying from the traditional ecclesiastical role of the monk.

stronger now than in the past. I have yet to find a university-educated or tourist Sherpa who does not believe in reincarnation or prostrate himself before the rimpoche to receive his blessing. If the prolonged absence of Sherpas from their villages continues, a time may come when many of them will have had little experience of Buddhist rituals such as Mani-Rimdu. This could result eventually in a weakening of religious sentiment. But in each of the three years from 1985 to 1987 an elaborate ritual (*boomtso,* literally "one hundred thousand offerings for the well-being of mankind") was held at Tengboche whose costs included Rs 300,000 for the performance and Rs 75,000 for a helicopter to import a renowned Nyingmapa lama. These funds, plus donations to the visiting lama, were collected from Khumbu villagers, despite a general

Fig. 89. Ang Rita stands by the window of a hermitage in the nunnery of Devuche; its occupant will receive food and water there but will not see or talk with anyone during a retreat that ideally lasts three years, three months, and three days. The window is temporary; it will be removed when the seclusion is broken.

feeling that the sums were extravagant and a financial strain on individual villagers.

To flourish, a religion like Buddhism requires full-time practitioners, particularly specialists who can maintain levels of purity and religiosity that lay villagers cannot possibly aspire to (Fig. 89). The danger to Buddhism in Khumbu lies not in the threat from other ideologies—indeed none seems to be even faintly competitive. The efforts of Christian missionaries to proselytize Sherpa students in the high schools elsewhere in Nepal have been ineffectual and even resented. The danger to the practice of Buddhism at its present high level (in 1989 there were twenty-five monks at Tengboche along with twenty-five novices in the new school) would lie in the dwindling numbers of monks in the monasteries (if the pendulum were to swing back once again), which could ultimately result in an insufficient critical mass of clergy. There is no guarantee the novices will stay, and three of the eight *thawas* sent at great expense for further studies at Boudhanath (see p. 94) dropped out of the order.

In the short run tourism is enormously popular with the Sherpas of Khumbu. Although an occasional older Sherpa mutters ominously about what the future may bring, even such mutterings in effect acknowledge the blessings that abound. Whatever misgivings exist are overshadowed by the knowledge that most Sherpas have never had it so good. But if it is good, it is good in the way that a political honeymoon is good—the course of subsequent events needs careful attention. In Khumbu the second aim of the government's fifth plan is not being accomplished (employment has increased, though not in arts and crafts) while the third (promoting regional tourism) is. But it is also possible to accomplish both aims and still leave a residue of serious problems (e.g., ecological, political) at the local level. One may conclude, in other words, that developmentally the country is fine; it's just the people in it who are experiencing difficulties.

The Tengboche rimpoche told me that tourists are somewhat like the torrents of rain that plague the north Indian states of Bihar and Uttar Pradesh that border Nepal: the floods come every year, and there is not much anyone can do about them. A dam is a good flood-control device because it can let out water in carefully controlled ways so that it can be used for constructive purposes—irrigating land or turning turbines to produce electricity. Building Lukla dynamited the dam that had held back the tourists.

CHAPTER V

How Sherpas See the Future

The preceding chapters make clear that the people of Khumbu face a variety of problems, ranging from energy, ecology, and pollution to education and the preservation of religion. The solutions Sherpas see to these problems and their assessment of the importance of the problems, however, are less clear. That the foreign observer may offer assessments radically different from those of indigenous peoples is demonstrated in the following passage from Nepal's official government newspaper, the *Gorkha Patra:* "These days the demand for paper has gone up so much that in the U.S.A. forest after forest has been cut down for paper industries, so much so that it is feared that the situation will come in the near future when people will have to stop reading or writing because of the lack of paper." This Nepalese view of an American problem appeared in print in 1915.

In this chapter I propose to use the methodology of "ethnographic futures research" to elicit Sherpa views of what their middle-term future holds.[1] Using the middle-term future—twenty years is a convenient figure—has the advantage of freeing the imaginations of those interviewed from excessive attention to the immediate future (this year's crop, next year's election, reroofing the house two years from now) while avoiding the remoteness and unreality of a time so distant that they and their children and their grandchildren would no longer be alive to experience it.

By eliciting alternative views of the future—asking what really counts in the long run—ethnographic futures research also dredges up and exposes present values that might otherwise remain buried and undetected. But this methodology has another aim that transcends the traditional arsenal of scholarly goals. That is, it is intended to extend the time-frame that Sherpas (and probably all people in the world) habitually use in everyday life. Bypassing current worries, those interviewed are free to deal more explicitly and intelligently with an array of pending problems they have not yet fully confronted or of which they have been only subliminally aware.

Ethnographic futures research is not as unorthodox as it may initially appear. American historians, for example, have often been concerned with the impact of earlier ideas about the future (the nineteenth-century idea of manifest destiny, for example) on the eventual unfolding of that future. Similarly, when anthropologists investigate the history of a culture, they do not study the past directly but rather people's perceptions of it. Ethnographic futures research does the same thing, except that it studies images of the future instead of images of the past. The cognitive phenomena investigated are the same; only the verb tenses change.

Ten adult male Sherpas were interviewed in 1985, all in the Sherpa language. I intended to include mostly "leaders," on the assumption that they tend to be more articulate and thoughtful, but I also wanted some representation of the population at large. The sample, then, like many anthropological samples, is neither random nor stratified nor large. The main criteria for inclusion were simply availability and willingness and the ability to respond to the admittedly peculiar questions.

The lack of women in the sample is a serious and unanticipated deficiency. I had not expected to field a full cross section of the population, but at a minimum I had wanted both sexes represented. In the event, my highly skilled research assistant, Ang Rita Sherpa, was unable to elicit serious responses from women, even after repeated attempts. It is an egregious information gap, and I cannot even guess what female responses would have been. I only hope that someone else will add the missing dimension. Even to the men, many of whom had considerable experience of the outside world and its peculiarities, the ethnographic futures interview format seemed very odd.

The normal routine in such research is to elicit, for any given topic, three separate future scenarios: first, the most optimistic scenario that can realistically be imagined; then the most pessimistic, but still realistic, that can be conceived; and finally the one most likely to eventuate. Informants should spell out not only the "end result" as of the horizon date but also a plausible process by which the present will become the envisioned future. The point of the first two scenarios is to stretch the imagination so that the final scenario will be more detailed and realistic. Most of the Sherpas, however, were unable to project three alternative futures and ended up describing only the one they actually expected.

Of the ten men interviewed, one was in his twenties, four were in their thirties, three in their forties, one in his fifties, and one in his sixties. None was truly wealthy, but six were of above-average wealth and three of average wealth; one was poor. Three had university educations, one had passed through high school, and six had little or no education. Two are wardens for the Sagarmatha National Park; five either work for trekking companies or own tourist lodges; one works for a hotel in Kathmandu; one is a farmer; and one is a *thawa* at Tengboche. All were born and raised in Khumbu; four live in Kathmandu much of the time and have had extensive experience studying or traveling abroad, but all maintain close links to their homes in Khumbu.

These men were asked to formulate scenarios for Khumbu twenty years hence (in about A.D. 2005) with regard to the following list: firewood (energy) and forestry; education; religion; tourism; Sagarmatha National Park; agriculture and livestock. The list reflects my own judgment of the areas in which the most serious problems will arise. Before asking their views on these topics, however, I asked each man to describe what he expected would be the primary problem he and his family would face in twenty years.

Although none of the answers to this last question expressed exactly the same view but rather varied according to the circumstances of the individual, common threads ran through some of them. Those who owned trekking lodges were worried that the government might impose unduly heavy taxes on their businesses. Those who had studied through the university level and who lived much of the time in Kathmandu were concerned that their children might not retain the traditional Sherpa culture and language after twenty years. Those with the most education—including the *thawa*—also worried about the quality and quantity of educational opportunities that would be available. Those with relatively low incomes expressed concern that high inflation rates would make it impossible for their children to obtain the necessities of daily life. These "indigenous" worries are almost wholly different from those that outsiders like me conventionally regard as the most intractable future difficulties. The Sherpas' sense of the future and their agenda for it are stubborn facts that planners need to acknowledge. The Sherpas' comments on the six items on my list, followed by my own in four cases, are as follows.

FIREWOOD AND FORESTRY

Most of the respondents had pessimistic predictions in this area. Seven expressed the view that in twenty years the firewood situation will have become very critical. Their fears arise from several current practices. One is the increasing trend toward more and more tourist lodges, where firewood is burned extravagantly in comparison with the traditionally spartan Sherpa use of it. Moreover, they do not believe that the government will provide any alternative source of fuel to substitute for wood. The increasing use of timber for bigger and more luxurious houses is seen as another threat to the integrity of the forests. Still another fear is that a growing population will exert increasing pressure on existing forest resources. Cutting across all these fears is the Sherpas' acute awareness of the slow growth rate of trees in Khumbu under both natural and tree-farm conditions. Finally, there is a sense that individual selfishness will exacerbate an already serious problem.

But these same seven respondents also feel that some fundamental measure, such as the introduction of cheap hydroelectricity to power electric stoves, which might then be made obligatory, could greatly improve the chance of maintaining the forest cover.

The other three respondents took a more optimistic view. They see the national park and associated conservation projects, whether established by the government or by international organizations, as improving the chances of maintaining and improving the forests after twenty years. Better management of the national park by more qualified personnel, additional tree nurseries, more conservation education among the villagers, increased migration to Kathmandu and other parts of the country—all these will work to obviate the catastrophe the pessimists foresee. The optimists, however, share with the pessimists the conviction that it is essential to find an alternative fuel, such as electricity.

Thus there is high concordance among the ten about the existence of the problem and the factors that will aggravate or alleviate it. The difference between the optimists and the pessimists lies primarily in how those factors are weighted and assessed.

COMMENT

Sherpas know that they are losing their forests from such everyday facts of life as the increasing distance to sources of firewood, the time it now takes to find it, and the decreasing size of planks for flooring. Their perception that an alternative fuel source is needed is well-founded, as are their doubts that enough electricity can be provided. The present hydroelectric plant in Namche provides enough electricity for light bulbs in every house, but Sherpas use fuel for cooking, not lighting. The electricity available now can power only seven stoves, three of those in the Sagarmatha National Park Headquarters. Moreover, instead of going to bed soon after dark, as they traditionally did, Namche Sherpas now stay up as long as the lights are on (until 10:00 P.M.) and thus burn even more wood to keep warm and to cook. The almost completed hydroelectric plant that was under construction for ten years on the Bhote Koshi near Thammu was completely washed away (along with fourteen bridges, stretching from above Thame to below Jubing, almost in Solu) in the Langmoche flash flood of August 4, 1985. Thus Sherpas have a realistic grasp of the fuel problem, possible solutions to it, and obstacles to those solutions.

EDUCATION

Everyone agreed that in the future, education will be a more central and critical feature of Sherpa life than it is at present. Those who are uneducated now recognize the importance of sending their children to school for at least a few years. Those who have received a basic education are determined that their children have at least the same opportunities they themselves had. Even those who envisage their children working for tourists want education for them. They see jobs in tourism becoming increasingly competitive in the future, with the better jobs going to those with some education and a good command of English.

COMMENT

Underlying these views is the growing belief that education is the single most important factor for the success of their children. The facilities the Himalayan Trust has provided to Khumbu children have encouraged more and more children to enroll in the various village schools. The

percentage of students who continue beyond the School Leaving Certificate is higher for Khumbu than for Kathmandu. Many of these students are supported by the Himalayan Trust, but many others are supported either by individual foreign trekkers who trekked with them or
their relatives or by brothers who did not have educational opportunities themselves. Everyone agreed that education will be a much more
necessary and integral part of society after twenty years than it is now.

RELIGION

Seven out of the ten respondents believe that after twenty years religion
both in the monasteries and in the villages will be greatly diminished,
if not eliminated entirely. One reason for this decline, they believe, is
education in the village schools, which will orient people more toward
the material world and away from "superstition." Such people will be
less likely to support the monasteries. Another reason is that people
will have to work harder and harder to maintain their families and will
therefore not have much time to engage in religious activities. Inflation
will also cut into what might otherwise be spent on religion. As young
people, including women, increasingly work in tourism, they will be
absent from their villages for several months a year and hence will be
unable to participate in or observe traditional religious activities at
home and in the monasteries. Thus the decline of support for religion
will lead to its gradual collapse.

Two respondents distinguish between the futures of lay and monastic
religion. They believe that lay religious activities will be weakened
among a better-educated population increasingly oriented toward the
"real" world. The younger generation will not have enough time to
watch or learn the traditional domestic rituals, and faith in spirits and
local healers (lhawa) will disappear. But religion that is institutionalized
in the monasteries, by contrast, will continue to flourish. To maintain
the strength of monastic religion, the abbot of a successful monastery
will have to be a well-qualified, skillful manager of the gompa. Only
then will the monastery continue to attract monks and elicit strong support from the villages. Without such leadership the gompa will suffer
the fate that befell the Chiwong gompa in Solu: the complete collapse
of religious activity due to bad management.

Finally, one respondent believes that religion will emerge a stronger
force twenty years in the future than it is now because as people become
educated, they also become alert to and concerned with preserving their

religious and cultural heritage. They understand the importance of having a religion and culture of their own, and they will make every effort to keep them alive. Religion will be one of the main beneficiaries of this effort to preserve traditional culture.

COMMENT

Implicit in all these responses is a concept of religion as both essential to the good life and problematic. Despite its central role in Sherpa life, religion is conceived of as a domain of culture with a life, and possibly a death, of its own. Points of view differ primarily when respondents are asked to consider what can be done to preserve religion, especially monastic religion. The desirability of doing this is taken for granted, in accord with the general twentieth-century movement in Khumbu toward a more orthodox, monastic, transcendental form of Buddhism.

TOURISM

Six of the respondents believe that tourism will have increased modestly after twenty years, but they do not believe that this growth will contribute much to the economic development of people in Solu-Khumbu. Tourists in the future will spend less money and will use the cheapest means of traveling. As more and more tourist accommodations are built, the trend will be toward more teahouse trekkers and away from contracting through the trekking agencies that hire Sherpas. Thus the few who own so-called hotels (usually consisting of unheated rooms with hard wooden beds on which the trekkers spread their sleeping bags) will profit at the expense of the many who help trekking groups get to their destinations.

Two of the remaining respondents are pessimistic and two are optimistic. The pessimists believe that after twenty years the total number of tourists will drop. They reason that the present economic recession (a Sherpa perception at the time of the interviews) will not end. According to this view, tourist travel will always be secondary to such needs of life as food, education, and health, and most foreigners will find it increasingly difficult to travel. Hence the future of mountain tourism in Nepal is not at all bright.

The optimists base their belief that the numbers of tourists will increase on their sense that the physical features of Nepal, specifically the high mountains, are eternal—and not only the mountains themselves but also their magnetism, their attraction, which will not be dimmed by passing time. Moreover, the government will continue to develop tourism by building better road facilities, improved accommodations, and so forth, which can only attract increasing numbers of tourists after twenty years.

NATIONAL PARK

Everyone agreed that after twenty years Sagarmatha National Park will be an effective agent in the preservation of forest, wildlife, and culture. But there is disagreement about how this will come about and what the results will be for the local people.

Three respondents believe that the park will draft and enforce increasingly strict laws to achieve its objectives, causing such inconvenience to the general population that gradually people will be forced to emigrate from Khumbu to survive. As the growing population puts increasing pressure on supplies of fuel and food and even on wildlife, the park administration will aggressively pursue its goals of forestry and wildlife conservation. In brief, the park will promote forest and wildlife conservation at the expense of the immediate welfare of the people.

The other seven believe that the National Park will be not only an influential conservation agent but a necessary one. They think that as the park's staff become better trained, the villagers within the park will themselves become educated to the park's importance and will cooperate to achieve its goals. Already the park's mass plantation projects have underscored the importance of forest conservation. The respondents suggest additional measures to ensure success:

1.   Recommend to the government and international agencies that electricity be generated as an alternative fuel in the villages

2.   Persuade the park staff, including security guards, to set more effective examples in conservation policy

3.   Convince the park staff to pursue forestry conservation more actively

4.   Make compulsory the use of kerosene as a cooking fuel for all trekking groups and expeditions

5.   Establish cordial, sympathetic relations with the villagers

COMMENT

Sagarmatha National Park was established with neither the advice nor the consent of those who live within its boundaries. Because it was not so much established as imposed, it has faced an uphill fight to restore the confidence of the villagers (see chapter 4, n. 11), a battle which the responses indicate is slowly being won (even taking into account that two of the respondents are national park wardens).

AGRICULTURE AND LIVESTOCK

There are two views on agricultural and animal husbandry conditions. The two respondents who are pessimistic about tourism are optimistic about agriculture and livestock farming: as the numbers of tourists decline agriculture and animal husbandry will improve since these occupations are the only ones that can sustain the population.

The remaining eight respondents think that in the future agriculture will not be feasible as an occupation for most people because the number of fields per person or per family will decrease as family size increases, and the amount of arable land cannot be expanded. Furthermore, the younger generation lacks interest in agriculture and animal husbandry because these occupations yield only meager returns. This generation prefers such novel economic activities as trekking and pays little attention to traditional occupations. A final disincentive to their pursuit of farming and animal grazing is that these activities have to be done in extreme highland conditions without the remuneration and amenities that tourists offer in such terrain. Thus young people will lose their hardiness, ability, and motivation to do this, and old people cannot continue it beyond a certain age.

Expensive and/or insufficient hired labor for farming activities will naturally retard agricultural productivity. Moreover, as the traditional manure made of animal bedding and dry leaves becomes more difficult to obtain because of deforestation and the decreasing number of animals, farming will be further discouraged. On this view, farming will not completely disappear, but dependency on it will decrease. Potato and buckwheat farming on the limited land available, however, and the use of male cattle for carrying loads will always remain a part of the local economy.

CHAPTER VI

Summary and Conclusion

When I first made the long trek to Khumbu in 1964, I hoped, like many Westerners, to find Shangri-La at the end of the trail. One night en route I dreamed that I arrived in Namche Bazaar to find a gas station that serviced the cars there. It was a nightmare: Shangri-La defiled. When I did reach Namche, I found neither gas station nor Shangri-La. Like Lévi-Strauss, looking for bare-bones humanity in Brazil, all I found were people.

We adjust to new circumstances very quickly. I was sitting in Namche one evening in April 1985 when, precisely at six o'clock, the lights (powered by the recently installed hydroelectric turbine) suddenly came on.[1] I was reading a book at the time, and several minutes passed before the revelation dawned that a light bulb was burning over my head in a village that when I first visited it was a two-week walk from the nearest electricity. Even that realization did not prepare me for the discovery a little later that evening that the faint hum I had heard during dinner was the portable generator providing electricity for the video movies (some in English, some in Hindi) that were being shown in the hotel next door.[2]

The transformation of the economy from one of mixed farming, animal husbandry, and trading to one with a heavy dependence on tourism has already been accomplished. The younger generation does not remember a time when the biannual tourist invasion did not take place. To learn what life in Khumbu was like in those days they have to ask their parents or grandparents. What they are learning in the schools will enable them to exploit the change, control it, and confront it on their own terms rather than be exploited and victimized by it. At least they will be in a far stronger position to effect their destiny with education than without it.

The link between trade and tourism was embedded in the cultural implications of trade itself, which was a centrifugal force, pulling the Sherpas out of their small communities and into a wider world. Those who became successful at trade gained substantial wealth without exploiting their fellow Sherpas. Not only was that wealth evidence of good karma, but it also provided the critical economic base that permitted investment in the opportunities presented by tourism. Thus tourism arrived fortuitously to take up the economic slack left when the Chinese shut down trade in Tibet. The Sherpas had a long tradition of dealing with and profiting from foreigners; tourists and mountaineers are only the latest variety of outsider to do business with. Sherpas do not admire greed, but they acknowledge it as a universal human trait. Tourism was a novel means to attain a traditional end.

The traditional economy persists alongside the modern but is also modified by it. In 1959 overgrazing was caused by the great influx of yak brought by Tibetan refugees. Owning yak herds is still highly esteemed, but in the absence of significant trading, people recognize their reduced economic value. The total number of animals has not declined, but their type and distribution and the problems they generate have changed. Employment in tourism means fewer herders to take yak to high pastures, so the number of yak has decreased while the number of *dzom* and *zopkio* has increased. These crossbreeds are distributed among more, but smaller, herds that graze, or rather overgraze, the land closer to the villages. Thus the highly specialized transhumance of pre-Lukla days has evolved into a more settled pastoral nomadism (see Bjonness 1979 and 1980).

Because of different grazing and climatic requirements, herders tend to specialize either in crossbreeds or yak, but tourism modifies this pattern too. Some of the rich and successful sardars now own herds of both animals, which they deploy to carry tourist loads in different ecological zones (Fig. 90). They use *zopkio* to carry loads from Lukla as far as Namche or Tengboche (almost half of Namche's 102 households own *zopkio*, which can carry the loads of two humans) and then switch to yak for the higher, final leg of the trip to the Everest base camp area, thus capitalizing on the divergent capacities of the animals in different climates and at contrasting altitudes. The investment in a *zopkio* can

Fig. 90. Pasang Sona of Khumjung, father of Pertemba, follows his yak, which carries gear for a group of tourists.

be recouped in ten round-trips between Lukla and Namche, and the only food the animal requires is the hay that it can carry itself on top of its load.

The national park, meanwhile, banished goats from Khumbu in 1983 because they were thought to close-crop the land they graze. This measure may have protected the land, but not the low-caste Hindu blacksmith (Kāmi) owners of the goats in Namche and other people too poor to own cattle.[3]

The animals that overgraze pastures near the villages also eat field crops growing near villages (see Mingma Norbu Sherpa 1985). These losses, connected to a loosening of the logic requiring that animals be kept away from villages during the growing season, are offset by the new strain of potatoes that produces three times the yield of the old variety. The cultivation of carrots as well as cabbages and other green vegetables and the purchase of rice, sugar, and eggs from the Saturday morning bazaar in Namche have combined to provide a more varied diet. So has the distribution of candy to children by tourists, resulting in an increase of dental problems (Pawson et al. 1984). The peculiar dietary twist of the Sherpa who drinks only imported beer (Heinekens is a favorite) instead of the traditional homemade chang may be ex-

Fig. 91. The lack of iodine in the diet causes several thyroid-deficiency conditions, including goiter, among Sherpas and other Himalayan peoples. Although goiters are considered unattractive, they constitute a class of phenomena (which includes cretinism) to which good luck is sometimes attributed ex post facto. Iodine pills and injections administered in the school through the Khunde Hospital have almost eliminated these problems.

plained as an adaptation to avoid social and chang-drinking responsibilities and the alcoholism and ulcers that go with them.

The distribution of iodine has drastically cut the incidence of thyroid-deficiency conditions, including cretinism and goiter, which once had an incidence in Khumbu of 92 percent (Fig. 91). In recent years, how-

Fig. 92. The hut in the background lies a few yards from Syangboche airstrip. It is run by a Sherpa woman (*left*) and Seti Maya, a Kāmi from Namche. Seti Maya was born and raised in Namche, speaks fluent Sherpa, and wears Sherpa dress.

ever, the Khunde Hospital has seen an increase in such stress-related conditions as mental illness, ulcers, alcoholism, and depression.[4] Dissemination of contraceptive devices has led to a lower fertility rate, and at least in some villages births are now slightly outnumbered by the combination of deaths (including mountaineering deaths) and out-migration.[5]

The economic shift to tourism has produced an incipient class of "tourist Sherpas" who nevertheless largely remain as culturally rooted in Khumbu as the plain dirt potato farmer. The new breed of Sherpa no longer wears sheepskin pants, but he knows who he is. Change occurs in the circumvention or shortcutting of tradition, not its elimination or transformation. Because of the time and trouble and expense involved, *dem-chang* (along with *ti-chang* and *pe-chang*, which have always been optional) is now frequently omitted from the sequence of marriage process stages. Instead couples go directly from *sodhne* to *zendi* at younger ages—and they marry even more frequently than before on a "love" rather than "arranged" basis. The frequency of Sherpa marriages to

Fig. 93. Although Seti Maya seems to be treated equally in everyday matters by the Sherpas and is included in bantering and casual horseplay, privately she admitted great resentment at being treated as an inferior. Traditionally Kāmis were not allowed in Sherpa houses, although that rule is now more honored in the breach. Intermarriage with Sherpas was also traditionally unthinkable. Having no marriage prospects in Khumbu, Seti Maya eventually settled in Japan with a Japanese husband, as did her older sister.

Westerners mentioned in chapter 4 is only a variant of this tendency. A far more dramatic and daring example is the recent marriage of a Sherpa woman to a Kāmi man, both from Namche, an event unimaginable as late as the 1970s and even now exceedingly controversial (Figs. 92–94).[6] None of this secularizes, Hinduizes, or Westernizes marriage; it merely widens its scope, initiates it earlier, and truncates its rituals.

Although Sherpas rarely commission the carving of prayer stones now (Figs. 95 and 96), they donate considerable sums of money for other religious projects, such as building a new *gompa* in Kathmandu that Sherpa *thawas* can attend. When Tengboche burned to the ground on January 19, 1989, Sherpas quickly organized an executive committee to oversee its reconstruction (Fig. 97). The rimpoche petitioned the king to remove bureaucratic obstacles to rebuilding it. New options, such as a larger, solar-heated *gompa* and the removal of tourist lodges from the monastery grounds, were being enthusiastically discussed. The

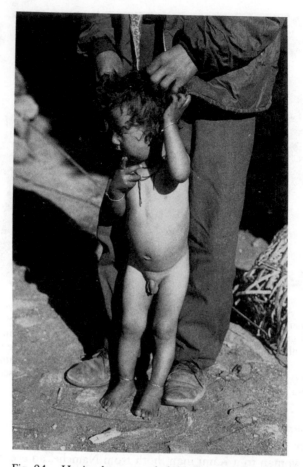

Fig. 94. Having lost several children, a Sherpa couple (the husband is a son of the artist Kappa Kalden) dress their son in Kāmi jewelry (anklets and wristlets) and give him a Kāmi name so that the god of death will not bother to take him. His status in Sherpa society is not affected.

Tengboche rimpoche has become such an activist for development (he sits on advisory committees to the national park, attends village meetings, raises funds for his cultural center) that the dividing line between religion and politics is less clear than it once was. More conservative Sherpas (including conservative monks) criticize him for these forays from the otherworldly pursuit of pure religion into the workaday, polluted village world. But he also cut a larger swath religiously when he

Fig. 95.   A prayer is being carved in this stone beside a trail.

became vice-chairman of the All Nepal Himalayan Buddhist Association in 1980.

The "tourist Sherpas" are conspicuous not only by their down jackets but also by the renovations to their houses. For instance, they have partitioned off from the large central room a smaller, warmer room around the hearth, using the remaining space for large gatherings and the display of large copper vessels (the traditional method for storing wealth) that line the shelves of Sherpa houses. This conserves increasingly scarce energy, as does the use of the few wetback water heater units (which heat water any time the stove is hot) that have been installed (Fig. 98); one-quarter of the firewood used on a traditional stove goes for heating water. The Tengboche rimpoche put forth an even more radical architectural proposal: to begin building smaller houses as a way of conserving heat.

Nor are the innovations only technological. In 1982 the *Dumje lawas* (i.e., organizers and hosts of the annual *Dumje* festival) of Khumjung proposed distributing uncooked (rather than cooked) rice to each village house, arguing that to cook such massive quantities of rice that must be reheated again later before it is eaten is a wasteful and inefficient use of energy. The notion was so controversial that it was not

Fig. 96. Tibetan Buddhism persists in Kathmandu, but this windvane-driven prayer wheel mounted on a Toyota is no guarantor of religiosity: the car's owner, Ang Nima of Namche Bazaar, was arrested and jailed for stealing an idol.

accepted, but the idea was broached and might be adopted in the future.

The efflorescence of monastic Buddhism in the last seventy years and the economic and political diversification of the last fifteen years have contributed to the declining influence of village lamas, civic institutions, and common village economic concerns and a corresponding rise of atomized self-interest. Those with cash—mostly younger Sherpas— have risen in stature and authority at the expense of the traditionally esteemed village elders (but not the very old, who were traditionally and still are concerned with otherworldly matters).

Fig. 97. Tengboche Monastery ruins after the fire of January 1989. Photograph by Bill Kite/Tengboche Trust.

Fig. 98. In addition to wetback stoves, solar hot showers, like this one in Namche, have been built.

Figs. 99 and 100. Pemba Kitar of Khumjung in 1957 (*above*) and 1974 (*opposite*). The earlier photograph was taken by Christoph von Fürer-Haimendorf, who used it on the dust jacket of his book. Although tourism and education affected the lives of many in Khumjung, Pemba Kitar's life as a farmer did not change appreciably over the seventeen-year period. He died about 1976.

My original hypothesis was that the effects of the schools on Sherpa life were minimal compared with the massive restructuring of the economy by tourism. But further reflection leads me to believe that it is the schools that are the crucial link between tradition and modernity because they have enabled Sherpas to exploit the forces of change (Figs. 99–104). Having successfully met the modern world on its own ground, these educated Sherpas have the cultural self-confidence to intensify their ethnic identity. The case studies of educated Sherpas (see

chapter 3) show that while tourism knocked the Sherpa economy off center, the schools brought change but also gave Sherpa society the tools to maintain its cultural equilibrium. Coming before tourism, the schools bought the Sherpas time.

There is, however, an Achilles' heel in this reinforced cultural identity. The Sherpas who live most of the year with their families in Kathmandu still observe, in modified form, some of the social rituals they observed in Khumbu. For example, rather than stretching Lhosar (Tibetan New Year) celebrations over several weeks, which would interfere with workaday business and government routine, a group of, say, fifteen families together rents a hotel dining room for a more or less nonstop three-day party. Similar arrangements are made for Phakning which, like Lhosar, is basically a social rather than a religious occasion. Both of these observances are innovative urban adaptations, which, as

Fig. 101. Lama Sarki, on the porch of the Khumjung school. He is the son of Chotari, the Namche climber who was the second Khumbu Sherpa to reach the summit of Mt. Everest and who later taught mountaineering to the Nepalese police. When I first met Lama Sarki, he was a student in the second grade of Khumjung School, to which he commuted every day from his home in Namche. He was also a reincarnate lama (*tulku*). He had spent a short time at his monastery, but, complaining that he missed his friends, he asked for and was given permission to attend school. He said he still preferred to study religion but for the time being would continue his studies in Khumjung. He graduated from Khumjung high school and worked for mountaineering expeditions (including one to Annapurna III) and tourists for a while.

Fig. 102. By 1988 Lama Sarki had married and opened a lodge in Phakding (coincidentally, close to his old *gompa*), a few hours' walk up the valley from Lukla. He and his wife stand in front of it. Although he has not followed his religious calling, he is still regarded as a reincarnate lama (as indicated by his name).

Ang Rita put it, "do not have as much life and charm" as their Khumbu equivalents. An organization called the Sherpa Sewa Kendra (Sherpa service club), a self-help group that assists Sherpas at critical periods—providing, for example, a proper funeral when a death occurs—also helps to preserve the Sherpa community while it adapts to urban life.

Sherpa children in Kathmandu, like their counterparts in Khumbu, are included at whatever parties, rituals, and celebrations occur, but without exception those who grow up in Kathmandu do not learn (or at least refuse to speak) the Sherpa language. Many of them were born in Kathmandu and have never been to Khumbu. Sherpas with school-

age children now choose a life in Kathmandu, if they have the option, because of the superior education available there. Their reasoning is that the curriculum and teachers have very recently begun to deteriorate in the Khumbu schools. English, once begun in third grade, is now started only in sixth, and the only teachers willing to come to Khumbu are those from other parts of Nepal who cannot find jobs elsewhere.

If a loss of Sherpa identity occurs, it will be among this new generation of Kathmandu children. Understanding Sherpa when they hear it but speaking only Nepali (and perhaps Newari) and going to Kathmandu schools, they are unlikely ever to return to Khumbu except for the occasional visit. They will instead become the Nepalese equivalent of the second- and third-generation Sherpas who live in Darjeeling—

Figs. 103 and 104.   Ang Tsering (not to be confused with the three other Ang Tserings mentioned or pictured elsewhere in the book) in 1964 (*opposite*) and 1978 (*above*). In 1964 he worked frequently as a high-altitude porter and retained the traditional long pigtails tied on top of his head. By 1978 he was working for tourists and had cut his pigtails. He died in 1985, in his early fifties.

still ethnically Sherpa but so far removed from the social and religious traditions of their homeland that they have become marginal to them. The roots of this new generation of Sherpas will no longer be planted in the potato fields and pastures and peaks of Khumbu, but in the cement and brick and asphalt of Kathmandu.

Appendix A:
Curriculum for *Thawas*
at Tengboche Monastery

The traditional curriculum consists of the following:

1. Learning to read the Tibetan alphabet (writing it is learned only casually, if at all, since monks are expected only to read texts, not to produce new ones)

2. Learning to read and spell words (the method is the same as that used in Nepalese schools; the English equivalent would be to recite aloud "a-p-p-l-e means apple, b-o-y means boy," and so on)

3. Recitation and memorization of prayers and incantations

4. Reading texts and interpreting, at different levels and at different stages, their meanings

In addition, *thawas* learn how to perform other tasks involved in worship, such as playing musical instruments and making *tormas* (dough figures). For more advanced studies, monks must go to other, larger, monasteries such as (formerly) Rongbuk in Tibet or (more recently) monasteries in Solu or Kathmandu.

Appendix B:
Khumjung School Curriculum

The curriculum for sample grade levels consists of the following:

First grade:	Nepali, mathematics, social studies, health, art
Fourth grade:	Nepali, Sanskrit, English, mathematics, social studies, health, science and hygiene, morals (morality stories, gods, Nepalese religion, etc.)
Sixth grade:	Nepali, Sanskrit, English, mathematics, social studies, health, science and hygiene, morals, prevocational studies (sewing, woodworking, clay modeling)
Eighth grade:	Nepali, English, mathematics, vocational studies, history, geography, panchayat and civics, science and health
Tenth grade:	Nepali, English, mathematics, education
Optional subjects:	mathematics, science, history and geography
Extra optional subjects:	economics or health

Appendix C:
Chronology of Solu-Khumbu

(pre-1950 dates are from Ortner 1989)

1480	Sherpas leave Kham, in eastern Tibet, for south-central Tibet
1533	Sherpas arrive in Khumbu
1553	Sherpas settle in Solu
1667	Founding of temple at Pangboche
1667–72	Founding of temple at Thame
1717	Sherpas submit to Sen king, member of a Hindu dynasty
1772	Gorkha (Hindu) conquest of east Nepal and acquisition of Solu-Khumbu from the Sen; taxation of Solu-Khumbu begins shortly after
1831	Founding of temple at Khumjung
1902	Founding of Rongbuk Monastery north of Mt. Everest
1916	Founding of Tengboche Monastery
1925	Founding of nunnery at Devuche (near Tengboche)
1933	Earthquake destroys Tengboche Monastery (subsequently rebuilt)
1950	First Westerners visit Solu-Khumbu
1953	First ascent of Mt. Everest (by Edmund Hillary and Tenzing Norgay)
1961	Khumjung school built
1963	Thame and Pangboche schools built
1964	Junbesi, Chaurikharka, and Namche Bazaar schools built; bridges below Namche hill and Lukla airstrip built

1966	Khunde Hospital built
1970s	Rapid expansion of tourist facilities in Khumbu; Solu Hospital and additional schools built in Solu-Khumbu
1972	Construction of Syangboche airstrip and Everest-View Hotel
1975	Creation of Sagarmatha National Park
1983	Hydroelectricity system installed in Namche Bazaar
1986	Creation of Tengboche Cultural Center
1988	Hydroelectricity system installed in Tengboche
1989	Tengboche Monastery destroyed by fire (January 19)

Appendix D: Recent Change in Khumbu

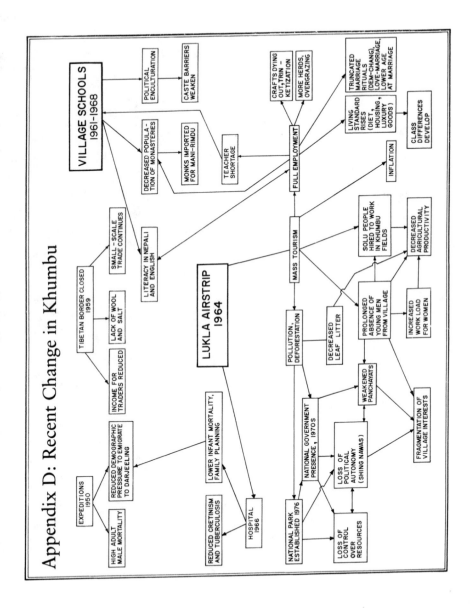

Notes

INTRODUCTION

1. Readers interested in more ethnographic, historical, or psychological detail should consult the works listed in the bibliography.

2. Even more research is being conducted in Khumbu now, much of it by scholars such as John Draper, Barbara Brower, Stan Stevens, and Vincanne Adams, who were already knowledgeable in Sherpa lore and language before they arrived in Solu-Khumbu.

3. A recent welcome development has been the appearance of well-argued reports by Sherpas, such as Mingma Norbu Sherpa's "Conservation for Survival: A Conservation Strategy for Resource Self-Sufficiency in the Khumbu Region of Nepal," and Nima Wangchu Sherpa's *A Report on Firewood Use in Sagarmatha National Park.*

1. THE HIMALAYAN SCHOOLHOUSE EXPEDITION, 1964

1. On November 21, I saw Hillary off at the airport. I was on top of the world until two days later when I learned, while walking down New Road on Saturday morning, of President Kennedy's assassination on the previous day. One of the most relaxing aspects of life in Khumbu, I found later, was not only the total lack of other foreigners, but also the total lack of news from anywhere else in the world. It took us a week to hear of Prime Minister Nehru's death, and that was fast.

2. I got to know the Unsoeld family well while I was a live-in baby-sitter for the four Unsoeld children during the three months Willie was on Everest. Willie died in an avalanche on Mt. Rainier in 1979; his widow, Jolene, now serves in the House of Representatives in Washington, D.C.

3. I was the last amateur to serve as Hillary's agent. The succeeding Hillary expeditions and projects have been, and continue to be, managed by Elizabeth Hawley, a long-time Kathmandu correspondent who has become an authority on mountaineering lore in Nepal. She now serves as executive officer of the Himalayan Trust.

4. Tem Dorje, a second-generation Darjeeling Sherpa, was principal of the Khumjung school and was also in charge of the Pangboche and Thame schools (both built in 1963).

5. We spent May 29, the eleventh anniversary of the first ascent of Everest, at Gokyo. Ann Wilson recalled how the 1963 Schoolhouse Expedition was host to a tenth-anniversary celebration attended by several of the famous old sardars. She said they had made an enormous iced cake, which Sir Edmund Hillary had discovered the night before and had innocently eaten a slice of because it didn't occur to him that it was for a special occasion!

6. In the flash flood of August 1985, when a ruptured rock-and-ice dam released the contents of a high glacial lake into the Bhote Koshi, both our bridges were swept away. I looked for remnants of them in 1988, but they had disappeared without a trace.

7. Details of the Lukla land purchases are given in the list that follows (on the date of sale, August 5, 1964, \$1 = Rs 7.6). The total cost of the land was Rs 6,350 (\$835.49).

Land parcel (in feet)	Price in Rs (with \$ equivalent)	Owner
160 × 121	950 (\$125.00)	Kami Doma Sherpani
96 × 169	950 (\$125.00)	Ila Tenzing Sherpa
240 × 144	1,050 (\$138.16)	Aila Sherpa
616 × 200	2,100 (\$276.32)	Tsering Choki Sherpani
159 × 222	1,300 (\$171.01)	Angel Sherpa

8. In addition to Ed Hillary, Jim Wilson, and me, the expedition members were Lyn Crawford, Don McKay, Peter Farrell, Max Pearl, Jim Milledge, John MacKinnon, Dick Stewart, Peter Mulgrew, S. Lahiri, and Brian Hearfield.

9. A film of a jet boat trip up the Colorado River was also shown. Ed thought it likely that jet boats could be driven fairly far up the roaring rivers of Nepal. In 1968 I went up the Sun Koshi in a jet boat with him. It was a carnival ride but not commercially feasible.

10. Dumre and a few other place names in the following pages (Chaubas, Chitre, Kirantichap, Chalsa) are omitted from the Nepal map for lack of space. They are no longer important to trekkers since the motorable road to Jiri has bypassed them.

2. A TRADITION OF CHANGE

1. The population figure for Sherpas in Darjeeling (Ortner 1978) may be larger now, but it is hard to tell since the 1981 census lists 73,589 Sherpas and Tibetans as speakers of a nonexistent language called Bhote-Sherpa. Even if there were such a language, the statistic does not include ethnic Sherpas who

list some other language—such as Nepali—as their mother tongue. The Sherpa Cultural Center in Tengboche lists 30,000 Sherpas in Solu, Langtang, Helambu, and Rolwaling.

2. For a Sherpa view of Sherpa history, see Zangpo (1986). Because oral history among Sherpas is relatively shallow, any account of their history is uncomfortably speculative. Detailed clan histories and other current ethnohistorical research by John Draper and Stan Stevens should ultimately produce a clearer picture of Sherpa history. See also the pioneering work of Oppitz (1968). Those interested in more historical information should consult the detailed, meticulous, ground-breaking ethnohistorical study by Ortner (1989), on which I have relied for many of the dates given in this chapter.

3. John Draper's view, based on his doctoral research in anthropology for Sydney University (personal communication), is that Sherpas settled in Khumbu for commercial rather than agricultural reasons. Or perhaps they were unable to take advantage of the opportunities in Solu, where the good land had already been taken. Khumbu may not have been entirely empty when the first Sherpas arrived. Some Sherpas say Rais kept summer settlements there, and stories are told of conflicts between Sherpas and Rais in those days.

4. Ortner (1989) reports that 3,450 Sherpas were counted in the Darjeeling census for 1901.

5. The present rimpoche of Tengboche, however, was trained in Karmapa and Sakyapa monasteries in Tibet as well as in Nyingmapa institutions. For details, see Zangbu (1988), 31–32.

3. SCHOOLS FOR SHERPAS

1. The Himalayan Trust has also helped to build or repair hospitals, clinics, bridges, *gompas*, and village water supply systems.

2. The Thakali students followed the lead of an influential leader, Hitman Subha, but his nephews buried him according to Buddhist rituals.

3. It would be equally interesting to compare maps by school-going and non-school-going Sherpas of different ages. But because Sherpas who have not been to school are generally unfamiliar with the use of pencil and paper and consequently have little idea of how to draw any kind of map, such a comparison cannot be carried out.

4. A comparison of the rankings of respected persons by Khumjung children and the *thawas* at Tengboche (a traditional monastery, unlike Laudo) would be tighter and more instructive, but I lack the relevant data.

5. The logic of the Cantril Self-Anchoring test is summarized from Nash (1972). Although the test may seem inherently ethnocentric, the children intuitively understood that the top rung was both literally and metaphorically "higher."

6. See Ang Rita's life history in the next section of this chapter.

7. The *kā* holds up the main beam (*dungma*) supporting the roof.

8. All reading in Nepal, whether academic or religious, is traditionally done out loud. Augustine's description of his surprise at observing St. Ambrose reading silently suggests that this practice is both long established and widespread.

9. These rather sweeping macro-generalizations vis-à-vis Hindu culture are not meant to deny the many contradictions within the society that Ortner (1989) analyzes brilliantly in her fine-grained treatment—for example, the strain between egalitarian ideology and hierarchical life.

4. A TORRENT OF TOURISTS

1. The discussion of nineteenth-century tourism borrows from Callimanopulos (1982).

2. Such a sherpa could be, say, a Tamang or a Rai, as well as a Sherpa.

3. Rarely do tourists enter Khumbu from the Rolwaling Valley (over the Teshi Labtsa) to the west (this route is now illegal) or from the Hongu Valley (over the Amphu Labtsa or Mingbo La) to the east. These are all high and difficult passes.

4. My discussion does not include the culturally conservative Thame Valley villages, which in general resemble Phortse more than they do either Khumjung-Khunde or Namche.

5. In 1986, ninety-four mountaineering expeditions employed 410 high-altitude porters (most of them Sherpas) and 10,412 lowland porters, but these figures include both Sherpas and porters who went on several expeditions and/ or treks in the same year.

6. The Saturday bazaar (hāt) in Namche was started not by Sherpas but by an army officer, because the expanding civil servant community had more diverse needs than the Sherpas. Hāt bazaars are a phenomenon of east Nepal; none are found west of Dolakha.

7. As evidence that at least some Sherpas do find the mountains beautiful, Charles Houston (personal communication) cites a letter to Tilman from the wife of Ang Tharkay (sardar for the French ascent of Annapurna in 1950) in Darjeeling. (See Miller [1965] for a discussion of the impact of mountaineering on Darjeeling Sherpas in the 1950s.) Recalling her Khumbu childhood, she writes of "those snow-capped hills and yonder mountains where our eyes never got tired of looking at the Majestic beauty of those mountains." At its face value her letter expresses an appreciation for the beauty of the Khumbu peaks; but it is also possible that she is seconding the view she knew Tilman held— that is, telling him what he wanted to hear.

8. Details on the founding of Tengboche Monastery are in Ortner (1989). Also see the Tengboche rimpoche's account in Zangbu (1988), 29.

9. John Draper notes that old Sherpas in Thame regard many current vernacular names as misrenderings, adding that young Sherpas are not aware of this.

10. Tilman (1952) reports that an Indian-operated rain gauge has been in Namche Bazaar since 1948.

11. Now that the park has been proclaimed a World Heritage Site, it has been given more authority to oversee development projects. At a community seminar in 1986, however, the park eased some restrictions and handed many powers back to panchayats. The seminar participants regarded the meeting as highly successful and significant.

12. For general information on Sherpa birth rates, see Pawson et al. (1984); for an interesting discussion of relations between tourism and medical practice, see Adams (1988).

13. An average of 3.2 percent of all climbers above base camp die; the percentage of Sherpa deaths, 2.6 percent, is lower, partly because some expeditions do not use Sherpas. Of the forty-nine expeditions during the autumn 1988 season, for example, seventeen (34.7 percent) did not use Sherpas above base camp. (In contrast, the Nepal-China-Japan Everest Expedition in the spring of 1988 used many Sherpas on the mountain and 1,200 porters and 250 pack animals to carry loads to the base camp.)

The 101 deaths on Everest (from the 1920s through June 1989) include those of 40 Sherpas (from both Nepal and Darjeeling). All expeditions in Nepal must insure their employees; the coverage for death ranges from between Rs 50,000 for a cook or porter to Rs 100,000 for a sherpa to Rs 150,000 for a sardar. In 1988 the Rastrya Beema Sansthan (national insurance company) insured 304 people, of whom 90 were Sherpas, and had 1 death claim. Oriental Insurance Company, which handles more than 50 percent of the trekking and expedition work, had 7 death claims in 1988, and 10 or 11 in 1987, including 6 Sherpas who were killed in a bus accident on their way to a trek.

14. It is difficult to give precise numbers for tourists in Khumbu. The figure 4,000 is based on records of the police checkpost in Namche, but some trekkers don't bother to register there. Figures based on permits issued (a Swiss team listed 4,706 in *Tourism and Development in Nepal* [1978]; a comparable figure for 1980 is 5,836) are high: many flights to Lukla are canceled because of bad weather, thus aborting in Kathmandu the treks their unlucky passengers had contemplated. Accurate figures may be somewhere in between, but I regard the Namche checkpost figures as closer to the mark.

15. According to John Draper, a Phortse man was recently employed for five weeks to carve stones in Khunde—perhaps another example of the pendulum swinging back again.

5. HOW SHERPAS SEE THE FUTURE

1. All other ethnographic futures research of which I am aware has been conducted with highly educated, Western, or Westernized populations. A full description of ethnographic futures research is contained in Textor (1980).

6. SUMMARY AND CONCLUSION

1. By 1988 a similar system for generating electricity had been installed at Tengboche; a fire caused by its unsafe use burned the monastery to the ground several months later (see Fig. 97).

2. By 1986 the park had adopted a policy forbidding the use of electricity for VCRs.

3. For the minority view that goats are scapegoats, see Brower (1987).

4. The information on current medical problems was collected by John Draper.

5. Sherpas who traveled to Kathmandu and Darjeeling had access to modern medical treatment before the building of Khunde Hospital in 1966. For example, the reincarnate lama of Tengboche went to Kathmandu for a smallpox vaccination in about 1941 (Zangbu 1988, 31).

6. Intense social pressure eventually led them to leave Namche and settle in Kathmandu.

Bibliography

Adams, Vincanne. 1988. "Modes of Production and Medicine: An Examination of the Theory in Light of Sherpa Medical Traditionalism." *Social Science and Medicine* 27, no. 5.

"Ban on Cow Slaughter in Solukhumbu." Regmi Research Series 11, no. 9 (1979): 129–30.

Berreman, Gerald D. 1962. *Behind Many Masks*. Ithaca, N.Y.: The Society for Applied Anthropology.

Bista, Dor Bahadur. 1971. "The Political Innovators of Upper Kali-Gandaki." *Man* 6, no. 1: 62–80.

Bjonness, Inger-Marie. 1979. *Impact on a High Mountain System*. Kathmandu: Sagarmatha National Park.

———. 1980. "Animal Husbandry and Grazing: A Conservation and Management Problem in Sagarmatha National Park." *Norsk Geografisk Tidsskrift* (Oslo) 33:59–76.

———. 1983. "External Economic Dependency and Changing Human Adjustment to Marginal Environment in the High Himalaya, Nepal." *Mountain Research and Development* 3, no. 3: 263–72.

Brower, Barbara. 1987. "Livestock and Landscape: The Sherpa Pastoral System in Sagarmatha (Mt. Everest) National Park, Nepal." Ph.D. diss., University of California, Berkeley.

Burger, Veit. 1978. "The Economic Impact of Tourism in Nepal: An Input-Output Analysis." Ph.D. diss., Cornell University.

Callimanopulos, Dominique. 1982. Introduction to "The Tourist Trap: Who's Getting Caught?" *Cultural Survival Quarterly* 6, no. 3.

Dart, Francis E., and Panna Lal Pradhan. 1967. "Cross-cultural Teaching of Science." *Science* 155:649–56.

Firth, Raymond, ed. 1967. *Themes in Economic Anthropology*. ASA Monograph 6. London: Tavistock Publications.

Fürer-Haimendorf, Christoph von. 1960. "The Role of the Monastery in Sherpa Society." *Ethnologica* (Cologne), Neue Folge 2:12–28.

———. 1964. *The Sherpas of Nepal.* Berkeley: University of California Press.

———. 1975. *Himalayan Traders.* London: John Murray.

———. 1984. *The Sherpas Transformed.* New Delhi: Sterling Publishers.

Geertz, Clifford. 1963. "Modernization in a Moslem Society: The Indonesian Case." *Quest,* no. 39, October/December, 9–17.

———. 1973. "The Cerebral Savage: On the Work of Claude Lévi-Strauss," in *The Interpretation of Cultures,* 345–59. New York: Basic Books.

Graburn, Nelson H. H., ed. 1976. *Ethnic and Tourist Arts.* Berkeley: University of California Press.

Gurung, Harka. 1984. *Nepal: Dimensions of Development.* Kathmandu: Sahayogi Press.

Hillary, Sir Edmund. 1964. *Schoolhouse in the Clouds.* Garden City, N.Y.: Doubleday.

Kunwar, Ramesh Raj. 1989. *Fire of Himal: An Anthropological Study of the Sherpas of Nepal Himalayan Region.* New Delhi: Nirala Publications.

MacCannell, Dean. 1976. *The Tourist: A New Theory of the Leisure Class.* New York: Schocken Books.

Mason, Kenneth. 1955. *Abode of Snow.* London: Rupert Hart-Davis.

Miller, R. 1965. "High Altitude Mountaineering, Cash Economy, and the Sherpa." *Human Organization* 24, no. 3: 244–49.

Nash, Manning. 1961. "Education in a New Nation: The Village School in Upper Burma." *International Journal of Comparative Sociology* 2, no. 2: 135–143.

———. 1965. "The Role of Village Schools in the Process of Cultural and Economic Modernization." *Social and Economic Studies* 14:131–43.

———. 1972. "Ethnicity, Centrality, and Education in Pasir Mas, Kelantan." *Comparative Education Review* 16, no. 1.

Oppitz, Michael. 1968. *Geschichte und Sozialordnung der Sherpa.* Innsbruck: Universitäts Verlag Wagner.

Ortner, Sherry. 1973. "Sherpa Purity." *American Anthropologist* 75:49–63.

———. 1978. *Sherpas Through Their Rituals.* Cambridge: Cambridge University Press.

———. 1989. *High Religion: A Cultural and Political History of Sherpa Buddhism.* Princeton, N.J.: Princeton University Press.

Paul, Robert A. 1983. *The Tibetan Symbolic World: Psychoanalytic Interpretations.* Chicago: University of Chicago Press. Reprinted, 1989, as *The Sherpas of Nepal in the Tibetan Cultural Context.* Delhi: Motilal.

Pawson, Ivan, Dennyse D. Stanford, and Vincanne A. Adams. 1984. "Effects of Modernization on the Khumbu Region of Nepal: Changes in Population Structure, 1970–1982," *Mountain Research and Development* 4, no. 1: 73–81.

Rowell, Galen. 1980. *Many People Come, Looking, Looking.* Seattle, Wash.: The Mountaineers.

Sherpa, Mingma Norbu. 1982. *Sherpa Culture: Way of Life, Festivals, and Religion of the Sherpa People.* A booklet published by Sagarmatha National Park. Kathmandu: Gorkhapatra Sansthan Press.

———. 1985. "Conservation for Survival: A Conservation Strategy for Resource Self-Sufficiency in the Khumbu Region of Nepal." Master's thesis, University of Manitoba.

Sherpa, Nima Wangchu. 1979. *A Report on Firewood Use in Sagarmatha National Park.* Kathmandu: Sagarmatha National Park.

Smith, A. 1980. *The Geopolitics of Information: How Western Culture Dominates the World.* New York: Oxford University Press.

Smith, Valene L., ed. 1989. *Hosts and Guests: The Anthropology of Tourism.* 2d edition. Philadelphia: University of Pennsylvania Press.

Srinivas, M. N. 1966. *Social Change in Modern India.* Berkeley: University of California Press.

Stiller, L. F. 1973. *The Rise of the House of Gorkha: A Study in the Unification of Nepal, 1768–1816.* New Delhi: Manjusri Publishing House.

Textor, Robert B. 1980. *A Handbook on Ethnographic Futures Research.* 3d ed., version A. Stanford, Calif.: School of Education and Department of Anthropology, Stanford University.

Tilman, H. W. 1952. *Nepal Himalaya.* Cambridge: Cambridge University Press.

Tourism and Development in Nepal: Impacts of Trekking-Tourism in Hill Areas. 1978. Zurich: Swiss Federal Institute of Technology.

Zangbu, Ngawang Tenzin [Tengboche reincarnate lama; Tengboche rimpoche], and Frances Klatzel. 1988. *Stories and Customs of the Sherpas.* Kathmandu: Khumbu Cultural Conservation Committee.

INDEX

Note: Sherpa names are alphabetized by first name and do not include the surname Sherpa (see the Note on Orthography and Sherpa Names)

Compositor: Graphic Composition, Inc.
Text: 10/13 Sabon
Display: Sabon
Printer: Maple-Vail Book Mfg. Group
Binder: Maple-Vail Book Mfg. Group